W9-CYG-818

PEN AMERICA

Published by PEN American Center,
an affiliate of International PEN,
the worldwide association of writers
working to advance literature
and defend free expression.

www.pen.org/journal

PEN America: A Journal for Writers and Readers
Issue 11: Make Believe

PEN American Center
588 Broadway, Suite 303
New York, NY 10012

This issue is made possible by the generous funding of The Lillian Goldman Charitable Trust.

Printed in the United States of America by McNaughton and Gunn.

Postmaster: Send address changes to *PEN AMERICA*, c/o PEN American Center, 588 Broadway, Suite 303, New York, NY 10012.

Email: journal@pen.org
Phone: (212) 334 1660 ext. 115

ISBN: 0-934638-29-2
ISSN: 1536-0261

Cover art: Tyler Bewley, *The Speaker*, 2006. Watercolor and collage on paper, 56 x 76cm. Used with the permission of the artist.

PEN AMERICA

11 | Make Believe

EDITOR
M Mark

MANAGING EDITOR
David Haglund

ASSISTANT EDITORS
Sara Crosby, Allison Devers, Matthew Goodman, Seán Michael Leahy,
Jay Baron Nicorvo, Loren Noveck, Elsbeth Pancrazi, Tommy Rudnick,
Lindsey Schwoeri, Eli Spindel, Heidi Tannenbaum, Justin Taylor,
Katya Waitzkin

LAYOUT/ART EDITOR
Justin Goldberg

INTERNS
Alex Aciman, Jessica Campbell, Kelly Stout, Sasha Tropp, Christine Vines

ADVISORY BOARD
Patricia Bosworth, Thulani Davis, Lynn Goldberg, Amy P. Goldman,
Neil Gordon, Jessica Hagedorn, Robert Kelly, Ann Lauterbach, Phillip Lopate,
Albert Mobilio, Honor Moore, Laurie Muchnick, Geoffrey O'Brien,
Ann Patty, Robert Polito, Elaine Showalter

WHAT WE BELIEVE

PEN American Center has a crucial role to play in these challenging times. Everything we do flows from the central mission we have in common with PEN centers around the planet, and that is to work together to sustain the literary cultures of the world. We pursue this grand aim with determination but also with modesty, because we share our work with so many others. With other human rights organizations, we work for free expression; with literacy organizations, we spread the essential skills of reading and writing; with publishers and culture ministries, we support translation and bring writers from abroad for our annual festival of World Voices; with other literary organizations, we recognize, through prizes, the best work of our fellow writers; and, above all, we share the task of sustaining literary culture with readers and writers everywhere.

PEN began in the shadow of the First World War, as European and American writers sought to bring together the writers of a world divided by ideological conflict and xenophobic nationalism. And the organization began, and has continued, by defending writers threatened with repression. As Chair of the Freedom to Write Committee of this center a few years ago, I learned about the powerful bond that links writers across nations in our common vocation. I often recall the words of a Chinese writer, to whom we had been sending letters while he was in prison. The guards used to taunt him by telling him he wasn't going to see what we had written to him. What they didn't realize was that he was sustained—as he told us when he was released—by the knowledge that other writers, half a world away, were thinking of him. He didn't need to read our words. All he needed was to know we were writing.

In recent years, as U.S. citizens have faced serious threats to free expression, PEN has been an active member of the community of those who have tried to fight back, especially through the Campaign for Core Freedoms. Our willingness to take on our own government—at the federal, state, and local levels—has always been evidence of our good faith when we challenge censorship abroad. Like many other PEN members, I believe that the current administration in Washington will be less of an opponent here than the last one. But governments will always want to control information, even if individual officials believe in free expression. We must continue to be vigilant.

While PEN members have always reached out to writers in other nations, our concern for the fate of free expression is grounded in a conviction not about the special importance of writers but about the centrality of writing in the life of every reader. We need to work hard every day to make sure that everyone who wants it has access to the rich worlds of poetry, spoken and written, and prose, fiction and nonfiction; to graphic novels and other literary works that use more than words; to drama on stage, television, and film; and to the verbal resources in print, in newspapers, magazines, and in digital media. We need to work hard to expand the numbers of those who want to explore these words we believe in, and to open literary cultures to a wider range of writers.

In the world of the literary imagination we are challenged to think about what we most believe in, taught new lessons, and offered competing visions of the true, the beautiful, and the good. (We are also amused, delighted, entertained.) Translation widens the range of the riches we have access to, opening us up to a world of cosmopolitan conversation. Of course, as Plato knew, poets (like novelists and journalists) can lie, and they can mislead us without lying. That is why a vigorous culture of argument and counterargument is so necessary. Wicked words, PEN has always said, need to be met with wise words, not with censorship.

When I was a child, in the newly independent republic of Ghana, my father was arrested and imprisoned, having fallen out with an increasingly autocratic head of state. Security police arrived at our house, looking, so they said, for "seditious documents." They began to search between the pages of our books, but, after a few hours, they gave up. We had a lot of books. "You haven't finished," my mother objected. "I want the President to know that my husband is innocent." She served them tea as they continued. (She was an Englishwoman, after all.) By the end, they were begging her permission to go.

Of course, what was truly seditious—at least from the perspective of an autocrat—wasn't between the pages of these books. It was on them. A concern for human rights, human dignity, the ideals of citizenship: These were nourished by dog-eared copies of Cicero and Dickens, Tolstoy and George Eliot, James Baldwin and John Stuart Mill. Our family was sustained, too, by people in other countries, people we did not know, who wrote to our president, to their newspapers, and to us, to denounce the imprisonment of an innocent man. Knowing they were on our side was a deeply heartening gift.

It's the kind of generosity that PEN members have practiced over nine decades. Often, we help obtain the release of detained writers. But even when we don't, we strengthen them, their families, and their friends.

As someone who grew up sustained both by the words on those dog-eared pages and by the compassionate words of generous strangers, I am honored to have been asked to preside over PEN's work for a while.

— **Kwame Anthony Appiah**
President, PEN American Center

JOIN US!

BECOME A CHARTER MEMBER
OF THE FRIENDS OF *PEN AMERICA.*

PEN America is published with the help of a generous grant from the Lillian Goldman Charitable Trust. We also depend on the support of PEN Members and other readers. This publication would not be possible without help from the supporters listed on the next page.

Since 2001, we have provided a home for literature that speaks across cultural, political, and linguistic boundaries. Please join us in this important work.

If you are able, consider supporting us at one of the following levels:

FRIEND: $100-$249
Friends receive a book by one of our contributors and acknowledgment in every issue of the journal for a full year and on our website.

ALLY: $250-$499
Allies receive a signed book by one of our contributors and acknowledgment in the journal and on our website.

COMPATRIOT: $500-$999
Compatriots receive invitations to PEN events, a signed book by one of our contributors, and acknowledgment in the journal and on our website.

AMBASSADOR: $1000-$2499
Ambassadors receive invitations to PEN parties and events, a personalized book by one of our contributors, and acknowledgment in the journal and on our website.

COUNCIL: $2500+
Council members will have tea with our editor and receive invitations to PEN parties and events, a personalized book, and acknowledgment in the journal and on our website.

Your contribution will be tax-deductible to the fullest extent allowed by law, and can be made by check or credit card. We will send you a receipt. Checks should be made payable to PEN American Center and mailed to:

PEN AMERICA JOURNAL
588 Broadway, Suite 303
New York, NY 10012

To pay by credit card please visit
www.pen.org/supportthejournal

CONTENTS

FORUM: MAKE BELIEVE

1   Imagine a book you wish had been written, either by yourself or by someone else, living or dead, real or imaginary;

or

2   Tell us something you believe about books—their power or lack of it, how they change the world or don't, what they've done for you or failed to do.

KAZIM ALI

I wish Layla Al-Attar had lived to write the autobiography of an artist in a time of war. To tell us what it was like to grow up in Iraq, to choose the artist's life, to paint the bodies of women. To explain how you continue as an artist when people are starving and social injustice makes the human spirit smaller and smaller, to explain what art is responsible for.

There are books that tell stories like this: *Sitt Marie Rose* by Etel Adnan, *Memory for Forgetfulness* by Mahmoud Darwish, *Shoot an Iraqi* by Wafaa Bilal and Kari Lydersen.

But really I wish Layla Al-Attar had lived. Because isn't it possible that the book I dream of actually existed? Lying now in the ashes of a house destroyed by an American precision missile, so precise it left the houses on either side completely intact, ashes itself, drifting across oceans in the wind…

RABIH ALAMEDDINE

I wish Bruno Schulz had written a third book, or a fourth. Maybe he did and it got lost. No one knows for sure. Many writers have died before their time, but because of the horrific manner in which he was killed, and the genius of the two books he left us, I never cease to wonder what could have been. Imagine.

LYNNE TILLMAN

I wish Jane Bowles had written a second novel. I wish she had been able to do it. It would have been, because I want to know more about him, about her father, whom she adored and who died when she was twelve, and also Cherifa, her Moroccan lover, about whom there were many terrible rumors, the worst that she poisoned Jane. Set in Tangier, where Jane lived as an adult, and Woodmere, Long Island, where she lived as a child, the novel might have Miss Goering, from *Two Serious Ladies*, return in both places as the great aunt of Bowles's father. Maybe Miss Goering would tell the family story, and Bowles's father would interrupt with his side of it. Odd characters from Bowles's actual and imagined life would come and go—Aaron Copland, Moroccan dignitaries, itinerant Americans wanting to get high with Paul Bowles, her husband. Paul Bowles would have many conversations with Cherifa, while they were stoned, about Jane, her philosophy, writing, and her adventures. Jane Bowles's real-life former lovers would wander in and out of the narrative, complaining comically; and the desert would draw them all to it in bizarre imaginary scenes only Jane Bowles could have written. Her imagination was sui generis. Jane herself would enter the narrative, to debunk whatever the other characters said about her. Her conversations with her father would reveal her as a child, her sad childhood. The novel would be alarmingly funny, poignant but anti-sentimental, and shockingly sharp-witted. Jane Bowles would have written her demons and trounced them brilliantly and lived to a very old age, knowing her name.

PASHA MALLA

I'd like someone to write a book presenting Sam Cooke's *Live at the Harlem Square Club* (1963, released 1985) as a civil rights document. Cooke played in front of a largely black audience, from what I understand, went back to his raw, unvarnished gospel roots, and ended by lamenting, "I don't want to leave you, I don't want to leave you"—as though stepping off that stage would mean returning to the white pop arena. It's powerful and unbearably sad; he would be shot dead one year later.

TERESE SVOBODA

I'd like to have written books that end up with pages turned down and underlinings, musings in the margin and not *Who is this?* A book with a concordance

(I like the trumpet sound of that). A book with a bird as a hero, not a bit part in Noah's Ark. Books titled: *Six Men Shopping, Women Who Weep Needlessly, Pets Aren't Us, Underwater Sex, Recycling Bras, Bite the Hand That Needs You, Bituminous Bitches*. Speculation always ends in alliteration.

My most powerful book was *Crome Yellow* by Aldous Huxley. In Sudan I paid our dugout paddler in pages of the paperback. He then rolled his smokes in them, rested, and proceeded to pole us further up the crocodile-infested Nile. It was about a forty-five-page trip altogether and nip-and-tuck getting each page read before he needed it.

ROGER SEDARAT

In a version of the famous story where Rumi meets his great teacher, Shams-e-Tabriz, the latter places the poet's books in fire then takes them out, unburned. This is to show how spirit trumps the letter. Because this tale of writing rings true for me in the twenty-first century, I reproduce it in a ghazal, offering a fill-in-the-blank couplet ending for the reader to find his or her spiritual connection behind the words:

> *Now burn your useless books! You'll learn much more*
> *In schoolhouses of desire taught by* _____.

DAMION SEARLS

Returning from his 1854 expedition to open Japan to Western trade, Commodore Perry stopped in Liverpool and asked the U.S. consul to "recommend some suitable person to prepare his notes and materials for the publication of an account of his voyage." That consul was President Franklin Pierce's college friend Nathaniel Hawthorne, who recommended Herman Melville. I try to imagine Melville's travel book about Japan, "that double-bolted land," as he had put it in *Moby-Dick*.

I try to imagine *Prometheus Unbound* and *Prometheus the Fire-Bringer*, the eighty-eight other plays by Aeschylus lost forever in the destruction of the Library of Alexandria.

I seem to remember a note, somewhere in my papers, about a thousand-page mystical Jewish treatise on the aleph, which is the first letter of Deuteronomy, but I cannot find the reference.

All the books Walter Benjamin did not live to write.

ARIEL DORFMAN

It was because of Julio Cortázar that I came to read *Ayer Ya Es Mañana* (*Yesterday Is Already Tomorrow*) by the great Argentine translator and author Eduardo Vladimiroff. "He's like a socialist Borges," Cortázar said one evening in Paris, passing me the book. "You'll like him." Like him? I loved it, felt, as I read, that Vladimiroff was mocking me, telling me that his words were more deeply mine than anything I'd written yesterday, anything I'd write tomorrow. It is set in a Latin American country whose dictator believes he can save his land by keeping its capital perpetually underdeveloped, exactly as it used to be fifty years ago, with the hope that nostalgic tourists will immerse themselves in the past as if it were an amusement park. In a city that grows more phantasmagoric with each page, each lost character, each twist and turn of the duplicitous novelist's rabid imagination, we follow the story of Solando, a fireman who is being stalked by a pyromaniac. Thirty years after Cortázar's recommendation, now that yesterday already is tomorrow, I can safely venture that this is the one novel I am sorry not to have written, I am sad that, hélas, I am not Eduardo Vladimiroff.

CYNTHIA OZICK

There is one work, and one body of work, that I'd sell my soul to have written myself (should there be any willing buyer). The first is that sublimely philosophical drama, *The Importance of Being Earnest*. The second is everything from the societally antic pen of W. S. Gilbert, of Gilbert & Sullivan. (With, I might as well add, this anti-surgical caveat: I'd very much prefer not to have to undergo transsexuality in order to effect this wholly metaphysical desire.)

WILL HEINRICH

I wish that I had written *Jorge Luis Borges: A Fictional Life*.

JAYNE LYN STAHL

I wish someone would write *The New Book of Knowledge*. The one I've been using is getting pretty rusty.

MEENA ALEXANDER

When Asked What Sort of Book I Wish I Could Make: Book filled with words of love in all the languages that flow through me, book made of leaves from a mango tree, book of rice paper tossed by monsoon winds, book studded with pearls from grandmother's wrist and bottle glass rinsed by the sea, book of the illiterate heart, book with letters scratched out so the truth can be told, book with sentences that melt when light shines through.

ALEKSANDAR HEMON

1. If I could imagine it, I could write it. I wish I had written *Lolita*, or at least "Spring in Fialta." A few of Chekhov's stories too. 2. Literature—books—provide access to the areas of human knowledge that are not available otherwise. Therefore I am interested exclusively in the things that literature alone can do.

AMITAVA KUMAR

In the paper the other day I read a report about kids and the ways they use games to imaginatively make sense of the real world. But that is no less true of adults. If we didn't immerse ourselves in books, how would we ever know who we are? I was a teenager when I discovered that if I could string together words describing the ordinary things around me, I was suddenly able to turn myself into a person who had a map of the world. In a way I was still a child and words were crumbs I had dropped on the floor of the forest in the hope that next morning they'd help me get back home. It couldn't always work, of course, but it was only words that helped me describe my darkness and my loss.

SCOTT SPENCER

Literature is perhaps the most demanding of the arts—demanding not only of its creators, but of those who read it as well. Unlike dancers or filmmakers or musicians, who ask only an hour or two, writers ask people to sit in solitude for days, for weeks, word after word, page after page. Now, with so many modes of amusing oneself, so many ways of gathering information and filling time, books have gone from being virtually the only game in town to perhaps the place people turn when all else has failed. Unless there is an unforeseen meltdown of the world's technological infrastructure, writers will never again have the cultural primacy we once enjoyed.

Yet, attempts to introduce experiences from newer media are a poor idea, I think. Readers might not want bells and whistles—they may come to books as a refuge from the flash and throb of the electronic age. Reading will be better served if we maintain our place outside the digital paradigm, and remain deliriously Luddite, our words as intimate as a whisper in the dark, the very thing that feeds the heart of our humanity.

NATHANIEL BELLOWS

Recently, I was rereading *Human Voices* by Penelope Fitzgerald, and was reminded of how a book, as a physical object, can make a reader's involvement with an author's work even more intimate and personal. I've read all of Fitzgerald's novels more than once, and whenever I find something that I appreciate, I fold down the corner of the page—the top corner if the example is on the top half of the page, and the bottom corner if it's on the bottom half. (When both sides of the page have stellar writing, I double-fold the corners.) Because I'd read the book before, there were many turned-down corners; and as I reread, I found myself folding and double-folding until the book became origami—each crease signifying something new and celebratory and specific, creating a three-dimensional portrait of my reading experience. Maybe it's because of the intangibility of new media—Kindles and iPhones and so on—that the experience of rereading this book felt so significant. But there was something disarming about how the physical components of the book seemed to welcome my participation and manifest that elusive mutual transference between a book and its reader: the silent acts of speaking and being addressed, listening and being heard, the feelings of being captured, remembered, and returned to.

FORREST GANDER

Books obviously don't make anyone better, more deeply human, whatever that might mean, more capacious of empathy, intellect, intuition, psychological nuance; they don't articulate emotional experience or frame concepts in ways that have made any discernible difference to the world—our whiffled clod of suffering and greed same as it ever was—except in one endlessly iterated particular case called, in various languages by various individuals, my own.

POETRY

CHILDREN'S GAMES

Mathias Svalina

BIRTH
(for 4 or more players)

One child is It & must be born. The It child enters the rowboat that sits in the playground & the other children cover the rowboat with a dark cloth or tarp. The other children spin the rowboat four times while the It child waits inside. Then they all stand still around the rowboat. The sun slowly slides across the sky, heating the metal jungle gym & heating the dark cloth or tarp across the rowboat's maw.

After the sun descends below the tree line, the other children spin the rowboat four times in the opposite direction. They pull the tarp off the rowboat. The rowboat is now full of tens of thousands of scorpions. The scorpions crawl over each other frantically, alarmed by the sudden light & cold air.

Each of the other children must dip his or her arms into the boat's maw until the scorpions have stung them numerous times. Then they must go home to their bedrooms & turn off the light & lie beneath their warm blankets, waiting for the twist of headlights across the walls that signals that their parents have come home.

The It child wanders through the playground all night, calling out the names of the other children, calling out the names of his or her parents, calling out every name he or she can remember among the cacophonous clicking of the scorpions' claws.

MOURNING
(for 12 or more players)

Half of the children assemble on the playground at an early hour after sunrise. They sit down in a long row to await the coming of their friends. The boys are painted red, & carry their pencils & their pens in their hands. The girls hug their textbooks, wrapped in plain brown paper, to their chests.

The second line of children approaches the seated children. They come to a full stop. Several children are singled out from the rest & march into the space between the two parties, having their heads coated over with chalk dust & raising a loud & melancholy wail, until they come to a spot equally between both lines. There the girls throw down their textbooks with violence & the boys fall upon the textbooks & begin to write their names over & over on each one.

One child from each line is named It & must approach the other line. By violent language & frantic gesticulations the It child must attempt to communicate with the other line but the other line does not even notice she is there. A second set of It children then advance, & beckon their own children to come forward, which they do slowly & in good order. Each line displays their name-covered textbooks to one another.

LOVE
(for 2 or more players)

One child runs toward the swing set while another child runs toward the kick-ball field. Then one child runs toward the jungle gym & the other child follows this child. Then one child runs toward the trees beyond the playground & the other child runs toward the school. Then one child runs toward the school & the other child runs toward the swing set. Then one child runs toward the slide & the other child follows this child. These actions repeat for an unspecified amount of time.

If there are more than two children playing this game then they must follow or run away from one another at their own discretion. They should resist the urge to follow whichever child is closest to them.

On cue both children tie blindfolds around their faces so that they cannot see a thing & they tie one of their hands to the other's hand & they run forward. They must continue running, despite the swing set & the jungle gym, despite the gullies & creeks that furrow the ground. They must continue running even when one child has fallen. They must continue running until the game is over.

The children may say that the game is best played when the teacher is not watching, but the teacher is always watching & making notes for the coming report cards.

PRAYER
(for 3 or more players)

A circle is drawn in the center of the blacktop & two children sit inside the center. Each of them closes his or her eyes. Each of them holds her or his palms to the other's lips & feels the breath exhale out the nose. Soon the two children breathe in unison. Soon after, the two children rise slowly to their feet, keeping their palms pressed to the other's lips. They spin slowly within the circle, stepping together in unison.

After they have spun around a good number of times, another child erases the lines of the circle with a wet rag. This other child then tells the first two children about the time she was in the Gulf of Mexico & the water was so warm that it felt like she was floating in the air & how floating there with her ears beneath the level of the water she felt that she could hear the whole ocean humming & how later, in the back of her parents' car, she could not understand why there were salt crystals covering her legs. If there are other children playing then each one repeats this story to the first two children.

The first two children continue to spin until all the other children have finished their stories. They then attempt to remove their palms from the other lips only to find that there is no other child, no other set of lips, no other breath. The school looms above them like the bones of some ancient beast & the teacher is hollering out to the child, moving her arms back & forth like scissors.

FICTION

WINDEYE

Brian Evenson

1

They lived, when he was growing up, in a simple house, an old bungalow with a converted attic and sides covered in cedar shake. In the back, where an oak thrust its branches over the roof, the shake was light brown, almost honey. In the front, where the sun struck it full, it had weathered to a pale gray, like a dirty bone. There, the shingles were brittle, thinned by sun and rain, and if you were careful you could slip your fingers up behind some of them. Or at least his sister could. He was older and his fingers were thicker, so he could not.

Looking back on it, many years later, he often thought it had started with that, with her carefully working her fingers up under a shingle as he waited and watched to see if it would crack. That was one of his earliest memories of his sister, if not the earliest.

His sister would turn around and smile, her hand gone to knuckles, and say, "I feel something. What am I feeling?" And then he would ask questions. *Is it smooth?* he might ask. *Does it feel rough? Scaly? Is it cold-blooded or warm-blooded? Does it feel red? Does it feel like its claws are in or out? Can you feel its eye move?* He would keep on, watching the expression on her face change as she tried to make his words into a living, breathing thing, until it started to feel too real for her and, half-giggling, half-screaming, she whipped her hand free.

There were other things they did, other ways they tortured each other, things they both loved and feared. Their mother didn't know anything about it, or if she did she didn't care. One of them would shut the other into the toy chest and then pretend to leave the room, waiting there silently until the one in the toy chest couldn't stand it any longer and started to yell. That was a hard game for him because he was afraid of the dark, but he tried not to show that to his sister. Or one of them would wrap the other tight in blankets, and then the trapped one would have to break free. Why they had liked it, why they had done it, he had a hard time remembering later, once he was grown. But they *had* liked it, or at least *he* had liked it—there was no denying that—and he had done it. No denying that either.

So at first those games, if they were games, and then, later, something else, something worse, something decisive. What was it again? Why was it hard, now that he had grown, to remember? What was it called? Oh, yes, *Windeye*.

2

How had it begun? And when? A few years later, when the house started to change for him, when he went from thinking about each bit and piece of it as a separate thing and started thinking of it as a *house*. His sister was still coming up close, entranced by the gap between shingle and wall, intrigued by the twist and curve of a crack in the concrete steps. It was not that she didn't know that there was a house, only that the smaller bits were more important than the whole. For him, though, it had begun to be the reverse.

So he began to step back, to move back in the yard far enough away to take the whole house in at once. His sister would give him a quizzical look and try to coax him in closer, to get him involved in something small. For a while, he'd play to her level, narrate to her what the surface she was touching or the shadow she was glimpsing might mean, so she could pretend. But over time he drifted out again. There was something about the house, the house as a whole, which troubled him. But why? Wasn't it just like any house?

His sister, he saw, was standing beside him, staring at him. He tried to explain it to her, tried to put a finger on what fascinated him. *This house*, he told her. *It's a little different. There's something about it...* But he saw, from the way she looked at him, that she thought it was a game, that he was making it up.

"What are you seeing?" she asked, with a grin.

Why not? he thought. *Why not make it a game?*

"What are *you* seeing?" he asked her.

Her grin faltered a little but she stopped staring at him and stared at the house. "I see a house," she said.

"Is there something wrong with it?" he prompted.

She nodded, then looked to him for approval.

"What's wrong?" he asked.

Her brow tightened like a fist. "I don't know," she said. "The window?"

"What about the window?"

"I want you to do it," she said. "It's more fun."

He sighed, and then pretended to think. "Something wrong with the window," he said. "Or not the window exactly but the number of windows." She was smiling, waiting. "The problem is the number of windows. There's one more window on the outside than on the inside."

He covered his mouth with his hand. She was smiling and nodding, but he couldn't go on with the game. Because, yes, that was exactly the problem, there was one more window on the outside than on the inside. That, he knew, was what he'd been trying to see.

3

But he had to make sure. He had his sister move from room to room in the house, waving to him from each window. The ground floor was all right, he saw her each time. But in the converted attic, just shy of the corner, there was a window at which she never appeared.

It was small and round, probably only a foot and a half in diameter. The glass was dark and wavery. It was held in place by a strip of metal about as thick as his finger, giving the whole of the circumference a dull, leaden rim.

He went inside and climbed the stairs, looking for the window himself, but it simply wasn't there. But when he went back outside, there it was.

For a time, it felt like he had brought the problem to life himself by stating it, that if he hadn't said anything the half-window wouldn't be there. Was that possible? He didn't think so, that wasn't the way the world worked. But even later, once he was grown, he still found himself wondering sometimes if it was his fault, if it was something he had done. Or rather, said.

Staring up at the half-window, he remembered a story his grandmother had told him, back when he was very young, just three or four, just after his father had left and just before his sister was born. Well, he didn't remember it exactly, but he remembered it had to do with windows. Where she came from, his grandmother said, they used to be called not windows but something else. He couldn't remember the word, but remembered that it started with a "v." She had said the word and then had asked, *Do you know what this means?* He shook his head. She repeated the word, slower this time.

"This first part," she had said, "it means 'wind.' This second part, it means 'eye.'" She looked at him with her own pale, steady eye. "It is important to know that a window can be instead a *windeye*."

So he and his sister called it that, *windeye*. It was, he told her, how the wind looked into the house and so was not a window at all. So of course they couldn't look out of it; it was not a window at all, but a windeye.

He was worried she was going to ask questions, but she didn't. And then they went into the house to look again, to make sure it wasn't a window after all. But it still wasn't there on the inside.

Then they decided to get a closer look. They had figured out what window was nearest to it and opened that and leaned out of it. There it was. If they leaned far enough, they could see it and almost touch it.

"I could reach it," his sister said. "If I stand on the sill and you hold my legs, I could lean out and touch it."

"No," he started to say, but, fearless, she had already clambered onto the sill and was leaning out. He wrapped his arms around her legs to keep her from falling. He was just about to pull her back and inside when she leaned further and he saw her finger touch the windeye. And then it was as if she had dissolved into smoke and been sucked into the windeye. She was gone.

4

It took him a long time to find his mother. She was not inside the house, nor was she outside in the yard. He tried the house next door, the Jorgensens, and then the Allreds, then the Dunfords. She wasn't anywhere. So he ran back home, breathless, and somehow his mother was there now, lying on the couch, reading.

"What's wrong?" she asked.

He tried to explain it best he could. *Who?* she asked at first and then said, *Slow down and tell it again,* and then, *But who do you mean?* And then, once he'd explained again, with an odd smile:

"But you don't have a sister."

But of course he had a sister. How could his mother have forgotten? What was wrong? He tried to describe her, to explain what she looked like, but his mother just kept shaking her head.

"No," she said firmly. "You don't have a sister. You never had one. Stop pretending. What's this really about?"

Which made him feel that he should hold himself very still, that he should be very careful about what he said, that if he breathed wrong more parts of the world would disappear.

After talking and talking, he tried to get his mother to come out and look at the windeye.

"Window, you mean," she said, voice rising.

"No," he said, beginning to grow hysterical as well. "Not window. *Windeye.*"

And then he had her by the hand and was tugging her to the door. But no, that was wrong too, because no matter what window he pointed at she could tell him where it was in the house. The *windeye*, just like his sister, was no longer there.

But he kept insisting it had been there, kept insisting too that he had a sister. And that was when the trouble really started.

5

Over the years there were moments when he was almost convinced, moments when he almost began to think—and perhaps even did think for weeks or months at a time—that he never had a sister. It would have been easier to think this than to think she had been alive and then, perhaps partly because of him, not alive. Being not alive wasn't like being dead, he felt: it was much, much worse. There were years too when he simply didn't choose, when he saw her as both real and make believe and sometimes neither of those things. But in the end what made him keep believing in her—despite the line of doctors that visited him as a child, despite the rift it made between him and his mother, despite years of forced treatment and various drugs that made him feel like his head had been filled with wet sand, despite years of having to pretend to be cured—was simply this: He was the only one who believed his sister was real. If he stopped believing, what hope would there be for her?

Thus he found himself, even when his mother was dead and he himself was old and alone, brooding on his sister, wondering what had become of her. He wondered if one day she would simply reappear, young as ever, ready to continue with the games they had played. Maybe she would simply suddenly be there again, her tiny fingers worked up behind a shingle, staring expectantly at him, waiting for him to tell her what she was feeling, to make up words for what was pressed there between the house and its skin, lying in wait.

"What is it?" he would say in a hoarse voice, leaning on his cane.

"I feel something," she would say. "What am I feeling?"

And he would set about describing it. *Did it feel red? Did it feel warm-blooded or cold? Was it round? Was it smooth like glass?* All the while, he knew, he would be thinking not about what he was saying but about the wind at his back. If he turned around, he would be wondering, would he find the wind's strange baleful eye staring at him?

That wasn't much, but it was the best he could hope for. Chances were he wouldn't get even that. Chances were there would be no sister, no wind. Chances were that he'd be stuck with the life he was living now, just as it was, until the day when he was either dead or not living himself.

MUST BELIEVE

ALBERT MOBILIO: Here in the early part of the twenty-first century, religious faith seems to have become increasingly prominent in world and cultural affairs. And this change in the salience of religious faith raises several questions, I think, for the art of the novel. If we think of fiction as "make believe" and religion as "must believe," how might novelists reconcile the ambiguities and uncertainties of their craft with an attempt to express or characterize religious faith? Is what is meant by religious truth the same as artistic truth? And if these truths are different—and perhaps they are profoundly different—how might a novelist who hopes in some way to characterize or advance the cause of religious faith serve two masters?

JAN KJÆRSTAD: The main point for me is that if you are a novelist you are first of all an outsider. You are going to be a heretic in some way. Everything everybody else takes as true on faith you are going to tear down, you're going to make it strange, show it from a different angle. If you write a novel, you create something much more open than a religious system. Of course, everything is a belief system, and the modernists—Ezra Pound, for example—wanted to make literature the new religion for a secular age. But I think literature can never be that. Literature is always the opposite of religion, for me.

BENJAMIN ANASTAS: I think there's a lot in common between the project of religion and the project of literature. Novelists may be heretics from belief, but if you're a believer, you're a heretic from reality. According to the Christian narrative, the world we live in is fallen. There was a time when we were in perfect lockstep with our creator, and we've fallen out of that relationship with God. The Gospel According to John begins: "In the beginning was the Word, and the Word was with God, and the Word was God." So the Word has a divine presence of its own—but the word has been separated from that presence. And we as writers, as keepers of the word, are now separated from that divine presence, in this view. So if you're a believer you look at the world and

This transcript was adapted from "Faith and Fiction," a public conversation held at the 2009 PEN World Voices Festival of International Literature.

say, "This is all a lie." I've been spending time with Evangelicals lately, and the more time I spend with them the more it seems to me that they look at the world with a Shakespearean fervor: It's all a world of seeming.

BRIAN EVENSON: I can think of fans who do pick up a work of fiction and treat it almost as if it was a religious book. It ends up being, for them, the basis for a code of faith. I had a very strange experience at a conference not too long ago, where someone came up to me and said, "Are you Brian Evenson?" When I said yes, he showed me words from a book of mine that he'd tattooed on his arm. And that really scared me. It's flattering, but at the same time you feel that someone has taken a literary object that had a certain amount of ambiguity and openness to it and tried to make it… something else. And I suppose we can say the same thing about most religious teachings: that as time goes on they become more formalized, less a way of opening up to the world and more a way of, potentially, shutting down the world. I am an excommunicated Mormon—I was very involved in Mormonism for a number of years. And I do think that being raised in that faith has had a dramatic impact on the way I think about my fiction and the way I think about the world in general. So it's a very thorny issue.

NADEEM ASLAM: My own relationship with religion is colored by the fact that almost every single person in my immediate family is a believer. And I'm not talking about my nuclear family, but about my eighteen uncles and my fifty first cousins. Every single one of them is a believer. And yet one of them is a gambler, one of them is a musician, one of them is a Jihadi. So I find it hard to pinpoint what religion is, precisely. I know people who pray because they want to connect with the absolute. I also know people who pray for extremely practical reasons. "God, I have an operation tomorrow. Look after me." "God, my daughter can't get a job. Look after her." "God, my son is a heroin addict. Look after him."

Unlike Brian, I have never been a believer. I realized at ten or eleven that it wasn't anything that I would need. But as a child—and this connects to being a novelist—religion taught me about consequence. If you do something good, there will be a consequence to that action, which will also be good. If you do something bad, there will also be a consequence. This is the idea of heaven and hell and what have you. And as a novelist, that's what you're trying to do, to take a character from a to b, and from b to c, and so on.

MOBILIO: I'm intrigued by this notion of consequence. One thing religion provides all of us with, even if we're not believers, is the idea of a narrative arc, a set of actions that take place within the realm of free will and have consequences. Jan, you studied theology, and I imagine you studied theodicy, the justification of God's ways to men.

KJÆRSTAD: That can drive you crazy.

MOBILIO: That's a good thing for a novelist—a bad thing for a mullah or a bishop, perhaps.

KJÆRSTAD: You can learn a lot as a writer if you study theology, because all religions, I think, have, at their foundations, great literature. The Qur'an, the Old and New Testaments, the Muhammad legends, the Buddha legends, the Mahabharata, the Ramayana, the Taoist small stories, the Shinto stories—they are so beautiful. And they seem open: You can read them in the way you want. But I think when religion came into the picture, people tried to narrow the interpretation. They said, "*This* is the correct reading." Then you get rules, and you have to behave in certain ways. When I studied literature, I thought, "I want to get into the business of writing things which are open." Umberto Eco has a beautiful expression: "opera aperta," the opened work—one you can read in one hundred directions. That's what you want to do when you write a good story. You want the reader to use his or her imagination.

ANASTAS: I think it depends on the religious group. Think of Judaism and the Talmud—that's layer upon layer upon layer of commentary. There's no one prescribed interpretation. What you end up with is a collective interpretation of many scholars and many experts.

KJÆRSTAD: Yeah, but that tradition is very special, I think. And when it comes to the practice of Judaism, they do narrow it down. As readers, though, they are very good.

EVENSON: Maybe we should not only think about fiction in relation to religion, but about criticism in relation to religion. We have these written works, scriptures, but the religions they found are based on what comes after: the ways in which they're interpreted and the ways in which they're narrowed.

MOBILIO: Well, I'm not sure I can accept the equivalence between interpretations of, say, the Talmud and *Anna Karenina*. Within a religious context, we're encouraged to approach sacred texts as the word of God, and the job of interpretation is to find the *right* interpretation. As contemporary critics or contemporary readers we come to literature with a different kind of belief: that there are many, many interpretations, and not a single one of them is correct.

But isn't the presumption for all religious texts that the sacred word is distinct from the fallen word? And is there a way, perhaps, in which every novelist aspires to that condition of sacredness?

ANASTAS: Sure. I was in New Orleans a couple weekends ago and I went to mass. I don't go to Catholic services very often. There's a procession, and the cross comes out, and the archbishop or whoever it is carries the book, which is covered with gold—it's beautiful. The crowd stops and the book moves through the church and takes its special place on the table. And I thought, "Wow! That's really how we should treat a book."

MOBILIO: At Barnes & Noble, for the front table, the sales person should bring the novels that are going to be placed—

ANASTAS: As long as we're still allowed to write in the margins, I'd be okay with that.

ASLAM: That is how the Qur'an is treated. You're not supposed to put it on the floor. The Qur'an is not the equivalent of the Bible, in that sense, but the equivalent of Christ himself. Christ was God made flesh, and the Qur'an is God made word, as it were. We were talking about different interpretations of religious texts, and the way these can be closed off. And that raises another point—the political use of religion, which I think is an important part of this discussion. The Taliban was supposedly created by Mullah Omar to save Afghanistan and glorify God; that is the official narrative. But the Taliban is a political and military organization created by Pakistan and sent into Afghanistan. Religion was used because it could be used—because in certain societies, it can't be criticized.

The chemistry textbooks I studied at school said something like, "Two atoms of hydrogen and one atom of oxygen come together to form one molecule of water: H_2O." But when the Taliban took over they said, "It should now read, 'Two atoms of hydrogen and one atom of oxygen come together *if Allah wills* to form one molecule of water.'" So religion—because it is so dear to people and people think that the tiniest diversion will take away something valuable from it—can be used politically. It's a very powerful weapon. That is why such leaders don't want various interpretations of it. That is why they said that *The Satanic Verses* is not just a book. It is a book that…

MOBILIO: It's blasphemy.

ASLAM: Exactly.

KJÆRSTAD: I want to contest this notion of treating our own books as some kind of holy business. I can't agree with that; I think they should be profane. Nadeem's mentioning the Taliban reminded me of a book by Amos Oz called *How to Cure a Fanatic*. Oz says that a fanatic should read fiction. Why? Because to read fiction you need, first, imagination—and you need imagination to have empathy. If you have empathy with people, you can't kill them so easily. Second, if you read fiction, you learn to be curious about things. And third, and maybe this is the most important, when you read good fiction, you learn a sense of humor. It's very seldom that you see a fanatic laugh. And you seldom talk about laughing when you talk about religious literature. But I think you should laugh. We should be jesters. What Salman Rushdie did with *The Satanic Verses* was that he behaved a little like the fool, the jester in the old days—and then it became very, very dangerous for him.

ANASTAS: I think you've touched on two reasons we have literature in the first place. A religious book manages to create, for some people, a kind of closed world, in which interpretation ends. And then this closed book is used for political purposes; something that is supposed to be of the spirit is used for the flesh. And people are outraged. So you think, "How do I tear this down, when I use the word?" You write a novel.

EVENSON: We've begun circling around the notions of the sacred and the profane. And of course you can't have anything that's profane without having a belief in the sacred. But, perhaps partly because I grew up in a culture that was very clear about what they thought was sacred, I see my task as a writer, like Jan, to be profane, to disrupt or work against the sacred in some way. But of course there is a kind of sacredness to that idea, too—an alternative sacredness, without the larger structure that keeps things in place and maintains the status quo. Ben, you spoke about the divinity of the word. I think that if the word can open us up to something that is beyond us, then the profane seems to be as capable—perhaps more capable—of doing that than the sacred.

ASLAM: Are you a believer?

EVENSON: No, I'm not a believer at this point.

ASLAM: Are you able to say why you are no longer and why you once were?

EVENSON: Sure, I can talk about that. I taught at Brigham Young University, which is a Mormon school. Before that I was a member of a bishopric, so I was one of three people running a congregation of Mormons. I had been very involved in the religion. When I was at Brigham Young, a student sent an anonymous letter to a church leader saying that my book *Altmann's Tongue*, a collection of stories, was evil and supported cannibalism and existentialism and those sorts of things.

MOBILIO: Those are belief systems.

EVENSON: Right, and equivalent terms—I think existentialism was worse for them than cannibalism. Anyway, that led to me being told that if I wanted to stay at Brigham Young, I would need to promise not to publish anything else like those stories. And I ended up leaving the school and later being excommunicated, partly by my own choice, from the Mormon Church. So it was a long process of faith being lost, I think, and I've gotten to the point where I've suspended the religious question. I think I'm probably as unreligious as anybody.

ANASTAS: How are you actually excommunicated?

EVENSON: There's a process for excommunication from the Mormon Church. They have a council of twelve men who get together and discuss your case, and you're welcome to attend. If you don't go they send you a letter saying what the court's findings were. And then with Mormonism, since Mormons have a kind of sacred underwear, called garments, they sometimes come and collect your underwear if you're excommunicated. I am wearing underwear now, yes.

MOBILIO: We've returned to the prohibitions that religion provides—which reminds me of the classic problem of Milton's Satan. That is, in *Paradise Lost*, Christ is not a particularly compelling figure, whereas Satan seems like someone we know: He's proud, he's vain, he's plotting to realize his own ambitions. When you think about characters you've created, does this come into play at all—this idea that the most interesting character will be one who is at the greatest odds with social and religious prohibitions?

KJÆRSTAD: Yes, I think it's much easier as a novelist to write about evil persons than good persons. Dostoevsky, for example, creating Alyosha—that seems to me much more difficult than creating Ivan Karamazov, whom everybody loves because he's going to stab someone and do whatever he wants. I wrote one novel about a mass murderer. And it was surprising to realize that a lot of readers loved this person. They could identify with this person. I wanted to give him many dimensions, certainly, but there seems to be something in us as readers—we want to create rounded persons out of characters who are negative and evil. That is why we are reading, in my opinion: We want to understand what it is to be a human being. And maybe we tend to know more about what is good than what is bad. But we have a potential in us, and when we read, we want to learn more about that potential. Maybe that's why we're more curious about the bad things.

ASLAM: I'm not sure I agree with you that Satan is more compelling than Jesus. I find Jesus a very compelling figure. I think that someone trying to do good is, for a novelist, just as important. And I don't agree that we can identify with Satan, who is plotting. I don't know anyone who's trying to plot anything. All the people in my life are trying to be good all the time. Failing, but trying to be good.

MOBILIO: But Satan, too, has failed. He begins as an angel—

ASLAM: But to say that that he's *more* compelling than Jesus—I mean, I can only speak for myself. You said that perhaps it's a greater challenge to write about someone who is trying to be good. But the way the world is structured it is so difficult to be good all the time. I think about the people from my own neighborhood, where the girls are taking up the veil and the boys are growing their beards. Pakistani and Bangladeshi Muslims who are born in England are becoming more and more religious. They're more religious than their parents. And I'm asked all the time, "Why is this happening?" Every day we have to make choices. Half of the time we make the wrong choice, we make a mess of things, and we have to live with the consequences of our mistakes, perhaps for the rest of our lives. But if you practice religion in a certain way, you don't have to make decisions anymore. Someone tells you what to think, someone tells you what to wear, someone tells you what to eat, someone tells you who to be friends with and not to be friends with, someone tells you who to hate, how to hate. That is why it's happening.

MOBILIO: Granted, the aspiration to be good is potentially compelling. But I suppose the problem with Jesus as a character is he doesn't have to aspire; he's purely good. And we might be drawn more to sinful characters because we understand sin, we know sin, whereas we don't know pure goodness. Jan mentioned his novel about a mass murderer. Certainly, Brian, your work is filled, as you noted, with cannibalism and violence and some of the darker human impulses. When you write about those things, how does it jibe with your sense of right and wrong?

EVENSON: Well, the funny thing is that in the New Testament Christ is incredibly compelling. The paradoxes of his teachings and the complexities of his character are really amazing and interesting. And then when you go to Milton's *Paradise Lost*, whether or not he's more compelling than Satan, he's not nearly as compelling as he is in the Bible. And that's a curious thing. There may be a certain kind of text that doesn't encourage depictions of goodness in the same way that another kind of text would.

I wrote a book called *Last Days* about a Christian cult interested in amputation. They take literally the passage in the Bible that says "if thy right eye offend thee, pluck it out…if thy right hand offend thee, cut it off." I wanted to think about how people would get these ideas, and how they would pursue them. I want to understand why people move to extremes—religious and otherwise. Jan talked about novelists and readers exploring what it means to be human. I think the fringes or edges of what it means to be human can reveal a lot to us about the more ordinary aspects, even if we don't want to spend all our time on those edges.

MOBILIO: Nadeem, you also have a character in your most recent novel who has had a hand amputated as a religious punishment.

ASLAM: That still happens in Saudi Arabia. For my novel *Maps for Lost Lovers* I created a religious extremist. She ended up becoming a main character. I had no idea she would. At first, she was the main character's wife. In the end, I pushed the main character away and she took center stage. In her last sentence in the book, she says, "it's not our place to say 'Why?' or 'How?' to Him; we can only say 'Help!'" I think we need to try to understand how difficult life is. There are six billion people on the planet, and we are the privileged few. Life is terrible out there for most people, and for many of them, religion is the only consolation. Go to Pakistan and see how life is there in the slums. You know, one of the big mistakes the Left made in the third world in the '60s and '70s—I'm talking about the socialist and communist left, among them some of my own family—was that they somehow linked the idea of social progress with the annihilation of religion. People were so attached to religion, and not for the wrong reasons—it was the only thing they had. And now many people of that generation realize it was a mistake to attack religion in that way.

ANASTAS: I think this has been a failing of literary culture in general. I interviewed Martin Amis once at his tennis club. There was the *whop* of the tennis balls in the background, and we were having a beer—it was a nice afternoon. He's rolling cigarette after cigarette and talking so much that they keep going out. At one point he looks up, very thoughtful, and says, "Well, there's no excuse for being religious in the West, is there?" And I thought, "Oh. He just doesn't get it." I was there as an American, and one of the things that has drawn me to learn more about religion in America is that, to paraphrase Fitzgerald, a second act in an American life can be really hard. If you fail, if you need a house, if you started out somewhere that was very tough to begin with… Life is unpredictable here. And maybe in some perfect world literature can help people through that. But religion does, in a profound way. And writers get things wrong when they dismiss religion out of hand. Religion means so much to people's lives, and writers should try to understand what it is that religion gives them.

ASLAM: Absolutely. And since we've been talking about books being open to interpretation or not, I have to say the Qur'an itself is not absolute, just as novels aren't. *Moby-Dick* can be read in so many different ways—but so can the Qur'an.

MOBILIO: That's true. But again, isn't it the privileged few who can look at religious texts with a certain distance? The people you're talking about, and the great number of people who do turn to religion for real solace, I think, can not necessarily pick and choose. I mean, isn't that what happened to you, Brian?

EVENSON: I think what happens with a lot of religious groups is they take a piece of writing and use one interpretation of it to gather people together. Think about a topic like evolution in the Bible. Is it literal or is it not literal that God created the world in six days? Once you decide it is literal, and evolution is a lie, you can get a kind of fervor behind that, and then you can use that fervor politically. So while many people turn to religion for genuine relief and support—and I think religion can be very good for many people—there's a lot that can come along with it, in addition to solace. And that's where it gets tricky.

ANASTAS: Well, practicing religion can extinguish the kind of inquiry that we need to make in order to write a good novel. I go back to a line in Galatians, where Paul says that "the flesh lusteth against the Spirit, and the Spirit against the flesh." For Paul, who's trying to go to church, it's bad. No good will come of it. But if you're a novelist, all good does come from that. It sounds a lot like "the human heart in conflict with itself," as Faulkner said. And that's really what literature is.

EVENSON: I know writers who are Mormons as well, and the ones who are really committed to Mormonism always run up against a certain moment: "Do

I want to say this or do I not want to say this?" Many of them end up not saying things because they're worried about it religiously. I think for myself and for a number of writers who come out of religious backgrounds, there's a moment when you make a choice about the degree to which the religion is going to control what you say on the page. And I think that's what separates writers who are representatives, really, for a particular group, and writers who truly do their own thing.

ASLAM: Are you willing to give any examples of some of the things that a Mormon writer might not be able to say in a novel? Have you talked to someone who has said, "No, I can't write that"?

EVENSON: There's a novelist who was questioned by church authorities because of the way in which she interpreted an incident in Mormon history called the Mountain Meadows massacre. She interpreted it in a way that was different from the standard notion of what happened, and that became a problem for her. She wound up being disfellowshipped, which is a step below being excommunicated. Another challenge for Mormon novelists is the sex scene. Mormons are encouraged not to watch R-rated movies, no matter how old they are, because simply watching depictions of sex seems potentially sinful or problematic. So, if you're writing about a couple in a novel, are you willing to write a sex scene if it's important to the work—or are you not?

ASLAM: Or you find another way of doing it, perhaps.

EVENSON: You find another way of doing it or you figure out a way to get around it.

ASLAM: In Pakistan, even if you find a way around describing sexual intercourse, you can still get in trouble. You could have a boy say to a girl, "Have you ever…," and the girl says, "No… " And that would be censored. Because the censors would see that as dirty talk—the characters are, in a way, talking about sex. Even though no vulgar words have been used, that, too, can get censored.

MOBILIO: This is perhaps another example where prohibitions produce the kind of tension that allows the novelist to thrive. Novelists, writers, and artists for centuries worked against prohibitions and censorship. Fran Lebowitz said that five hundred years of the oppression of homosexuals had yielded the Sistine Chapel and Oscar Wilde, whereas ten years—she was speaking in the 1970s—ten years of gay liberation had yielded leather underwear.

EVENSON: Nothing against leather underwear.

MOBILIO: Or sacred garments. But certainly in the past hundred or hundred and fifty years, artists and writers have more explicitly dealt with human beings as sexual beings, and this is one reason artists and novelists have come head to head with religious scripture. In *The Wasted Vigil*, there's a powerful scene where—well, Nadeem, let me have you describe what happens.

ASLAM: The book is set in Afghanistan. I went to that country and to the now troubled areas of Pakistan. I was riding a bus and I just started talking to the chap I was sitting next to. When I told him I was writing a novel about Pakistan, he grinned and said, "Shall I tell you something?" I said yes, and he said, "I went to a terrorist training camp." He then told me that, until the age of thirteen, he hadn't seen a woman, because he grew up in an orphanage in Afghanistan, then he went to a madrassa, and after that he ended up in the camp. And he said that while he was at the camp, he heard a rumor that one of the other boys had a photograph of a woman's face. If the boy was found out, he'd have gotten in trouble, because Islam, according to the Islamists, forbids photography. So the boys cut the photograph up into small pieces and hid the pieces in various places in the camp. Once a month, all the pieces would be brought together like a jigsaw and they would have a viewing party. And he said, "I begged them to let me see it, and eventually they invited me to this secret place. The first time I saw the woman I fainted, because I could not believe that this thing could exist." Then he told me about one of their friends who died in a training exercise. They were out on the hills and he was very tired and he slipped and fell into the ravine and died. And this young man said, "We actually buried one of the woman's eyes with him because he loved her so much." I took that a step further in the novel—the boys now want the eye back because the girl looks strange without the eye. So they actually go into the grave and fish it out.

MOBILIO: What a story. I think on that note we might want to ask the audience if they have any questions.

AUDIENCE: I was raised a fundamentalist Christian, and had the privilege of being banned from Bob Jones University; because I'm gay, they would not allow me back on the campus again. But that's another story. I spent quite a few years kind of deprogramming myself from the religion by being what I would call "purposefully bad," and exploring badness, because I was always taught this extreme form of being good. And I considered these two things to be related—

being an artist and a writer and being bad, somehow. As the years have gone by, I have thought more and more about fundamentalism and its exclusionary premise: It exists by excluding everything else but itself. And I have come to appreciate that idea—not in the way that they use it, but in the way it allows me to locate myself outside of something, to be the outsider, as Jan was saying. This pulling away from the world seems quite necessary for the artist if he wants to say something about it. I'm mostly thinking of Brian with this question. Do you see any weird benefit as an artist to being raised in a very particularly defined religious manner?

EVENSON: I do think it's had a huge impact on me, being raised Mormon. I think it's made me a little strange. But I also think that I grew up with a very firm sense of consequence, as Nadeem said. A lot of my ethical responses to things come pretty directly out of Mormonism, though they've been modified in ways that Mormons might not recognize. And there is something else about having a religious structure that you grow up in relation to: When you leave the religion, that structure starts to open up, and you see it in a new way. When I was a student at Brigham Young University, I remember they did this thing at eight o'clock in the morning and then five o'clock at night. They raise and lower the American flag. And when they do that they blast the national anthem, I think it is—I don't remember for sure. Maybe I've blacked it out. But everyone on campus, whether they could see the flag or not, would stop and put their hands over their hearts, and they would face wherever they thought the flag would be if they could actually see it. If you kept walking, people really gave you dirty looks, but you felt like you were gaining this incredible amount of time. It's like you had stepped outside of time. It used to make me incredibly happy to walk right then.

ASLAM: I don't really want to be an outsider. I want to observe things from the inside. As an artist, I would like to be invisible, but not an outsider. I've just come back from Pakistan. And I wear this ring, which is from one of the Muslim saints, a gay saint, who was so loathed by the clergy that when he died, they refused to bury him. And the people pushed the mullahs aside and buried the saint themselves, and now thousands of men and women and children travel to his grave. He's the patron saint of lovers. Now I wear this ring on the left hand. At the Islamabad airport, a chap came up to me and said, "Excuse me, I hope you don't mind, but that is a sacred ring. Is it from Lahore?" I said, "Yes, it is." And he said that the left hand in Islam is considered a dirty thing. "It would be better if you wore it on your clean hand, because it is a sacred ring." Well, I don't make any distinction between right hand and left. But I took the ring off and, for the rest of my time in Pakistan, I wore it on the right hand. I mean, why hurt someone? Now, when I came back to London, I realized that the ring I was wearing was one I bought in Barcelona—it just looks like the ring I bought in Lahore. But even if I had known at the airport that this was the ring from Barcelona, I would've worn it on the right hand, because it looks like the ring that I bought in Lahore. And I'm not trying to antagonize anyone. You could say, if you knew that this ring was from Barcelona, you could have expanded the man's horizons. You could have said, "Dude! Not every ring that looks like this is from Lahore. I am from the West," etc. I could have had a conversation with him. You could say that the man would have learned something. But I don't pursue such confrontations.

MOBILIO: That is certainly one of the criticisms leveled at Salman Rushdie. Why antagonize?

ASLAM: No, no, if he wants to do that, he should. But I think one needs to decide such things case by case. The idea that an artist *must* be an outsider has never really connected with me.

ANASTAS: But I do think in some ways the artist needs to get away from something, in a sense—and that something might be a closed community, or it might be something else. I was reading Susan Sontag's journals, which are totally fascinating. On the first page, when she's fourteen, she writes, "I believe." And the first thing she believes is that there's no personal God or life after death. But she goes to Berkeley, and, at seventeen, she has her first night going to gay bars. People are making out with her, and she ends up making out with this woman she has a crush on—it's an incredible, breathless passage about going from bar to bar. The next day she's reflecting on it, and she says, "There is nothing, nothing that stops me from doing anything except myself." This is a huge realization for her. And it wasn't as though she came from a fundamentalist background—that's not what made her feel like something stood between her and who she wanted to be. But something was there. And then her response to this realization, the last line in the passage, is, "God, living is enormous!"

AUDIENCE: One of the things that has come up in everyone's comments, it seems, is that as an artist one should treat any kind of certainty or assurance with skepticism. And yet sometimes the talk has danced around a kind of certainty or assurance about where we should stand vis-à-vis religion. And it seems like an unfair fight when you set the rarest and most fine and beautiful examples of literature and fiction up against the worst and most common uses of religion. You get this picture of religion as hostile to questions, as violent, armed with political oppression, and so on, versus *Moby-Dick*. And yet the five million people who read *Moby-Dick* in classrooms every year are mostly trained to say, "*Moby-Dick* means x." In other words, I think there's a mistake in accepting the fundamentalist's insistence that there is only one way to believe. What would you say to the idea of fundamentalism not as an opposition to great literature, but as an example of bad reading and bad writing—the kind of junk fiction that fills our bookshelves? Saddam Hussein was a novelist, after all.

EVENSON: I grew up in southern Utah, where there's a university. And most of the people are Mormon, but many of them have been out in the world and thought about a lot of things and are very intellectual. And as I was developing as an artist and thinking about the issues we've discussed, the question I came to was, "Is there a way to be within this religious system and still be a productive artist or not?" And I know people who stayed in the religion and have gone on to do interesting work. I just couldn't, for various reasons—partly because I was on the church's radar, so to speak, and partly because my own sense of my beliefs changed. I think there are people who are religious in a complicated way, and I agree that there are all sorts of ways to be religious. That's something Nadeem was saying earlier. There are all sorts of ways to approach religion. Fundamentalism is the most visible way, but there are other ways, too.

ASLAM: I feel a certain responsibility that I should be careful with the religion I come from, even though I am not a believer. It does seem to be in the news every day. If you study the statements of Osama bin Laden and al-Zawahiri and others like them, you'll see that they are in torment over the fact that the world has managed to make a distinction between Islamists and other Muslims. I don't agree with many things President Bush did in his time in the White House, but one of the good things he did was that, immediately after 9/11, he took off his shoes and went into a mosque in Washington, as a way of sending a message to the bigots in America. A gentleman had been shot dead by angry Americans as retaliation for 9/11. So the message was, "Look, the people who flew those planes into those office buildings had nothing to do with people who come into this mosque. We need to make a distinction." Al Qaeda wanted the world to stand up and say what Martin Amis obligingly suggested, which was, "Maybe we should stop every Muslim at every airport," etc. Which plays into the Taliban's hands. We need to pay attention to who's interpreting what text in what way.

MOBILIO: I wonder, Ben, your novel *The Faithful Narrative of a Pastor's Disappearance*, which quite candidly rips off Jonathan Edwards's title ...

ANASTAS: "A Faithful Narrative of the Surprising Work of God in the Conversion of Many Hundred Souls in Northampton, Massachusetts."

MOBILIO: I didn't have all of that at my immediate disposal. But am I wrong to think of that novel of yours as a satire of New England Protestantism and the suburban ethical code that flows from that belief system and that religious practice? I wonder to what degree the satiric mode is not the twentieth and twenty-first century's default mode for the artist when thinking about religion.

ANASTAS: That novel in particular exists in an uneasy middle ground between that idea of what literature does with religion—satirize it for its faults and for its hypocrisy and for the way the flesh rules the church—and another idea, which is actually trying to make sense of faith. Faith is the substance of things hopeful and the evidence of things not seen. How do you depict that in narrative? With letters on the page and sentences that turn into paragraphs and images that come alive in readers' minds. How do you make that essential mystery manifest?

MOBILIO: But novels do conjure the unseen—all art could be said to do that. Or perhaps the novelist works more along the lines of, say, scientists, or is at least approximating the scientific method, by asking questions and then, through the process of writing fiction, getting at some answers?

ANASTAS: No.

MOBILIO: No? Tell me why.

ANASTAS: That's the misconception that I was under when I started writing that novel. By the time I got to the end I realized, "Oh, no. The questions don't stop. They only really just begin."

The screaming of the children, which hitherto he had not heard and which now suddenly pierced his ears, chased him away, and he tottered like a top under a clumsy whip.

FRIEND

Kabir

Translated by Arvind Krishna Mehrotra

Friend,
You had one life
And you blew it.

From sticky spunk
To human shape,
You spent ten months
In your mother's womb,
Blocked off from the world
Into which you fell
The minute you were born.
A child once,
You're an old man now.
What has happened has happened.
Crying won't help
When death already
Has you by the balls.
It's counting your breaths,
Waiting.

The world's a gambler's den, says Kabir.
You can't be too careful.

Arvind Krishna Mehrotra's translations of Kabir were supported in part by the PEN Translation Fund.

IT'S A MESS

Kabir

Translated by Arvind Krishna Mehrotra

It's a mess,
But you're there
To sort it out.

Cock of the walk,
In great shape,
Keeping the best
Company:
That's me.

Listen, says Kabir,
I have a prayer to make.
I'm handcuffed to death.
Throw me the key.

FICTION

THE ANTHOLOGY OF SMALL HOMES

Sara Majka

There I was one afternoon, stumbling from the back door of the bookstore, blinded by the October light, and there, down a slope of grass, sat Nigel. He was at a metal table, a stack of books in front of him, his legs crossed, one hand holding a book, the other resting near a cup of tea. Some sort of broken arbor hovered above him, with filthy canvas flapping in the wind.

When I asked about the tea, he expressed frustration with the books he had found, outlining the trouble with each before sweeping a hand across the view, adding thoughts on postmodernism, nihilism, and the void, then settling on a barn in the distance. That color, he said, those silver planks. He was looking at the barn, but his gaze didn't fix; it seemed to go further ahead and deeper inside at the same moment. His eyes were a fine blue, but the whites were discolored, murky, with webs of red veins.

He shook his head and looked at me. Yes, he said. You asked about the tea? Yes, the tea.

The tea, he repeated, sit, okay? I'll get you some.

He stood and drifted towards the house. His movements always seemed without purpose. He was walking to get tea, and at some moment he would probably return with a cup, though often he'd forget. He would stop at a shelf of books, only to return later with no memory of tea, not even a memory that there should have been a memory. He would look at me startled as if to ask, *Where am I? What is it, what am I supposed to remember?* It was as if the rear of every moment contained a sudden fright that made him forget the front half.

I went looking for him, and found him back at the patio. A cup of tea in a white plastic cup sat next to the books, but it was impossible to tell if it was the same cup or a different one. He lifted the book I held in my hand, *The Anthology of Small Homes*, and began to laugh, Yes, he said, it is essential, these anthologies, one must always anthologize, and good to have those who read such anthologizations, but then he stopped laughing. I had begun, I fear, to bite my lip. Shall we go? he asked.

Yes, I think so, yes, I said, and later, in the car, my bony fingers clutched the wheel, my eyes hovered over it. When Nigel hired me not long after I had left the hospital—I still remember how he watched the quivering of my hands—he was mostly interested in whether I could drive, for he had lost that ability during a long and ambiguous illness. I drove with my face so close to the wheel my chin almost rested on it. (Like you are searching for icebergs, he had once said, as if at any moment, icebergs! To the right! *Catastrophe awaits at any moment*, I had said. Surely, Nora, you don't think that? *Perhaps it's from being so small.* Perhaps yes, he said, perhaps the small ones have it differently.) I turned to look at him, but his eyes were closed, his head rested on the back of the seat, flashes of light moved across his face.

Maybe my fascination with smallness, with miniatures, made me pull *The Anthology of Small Homes* from the shelf of the bookstore. I could hardly say how it occurred to me. I was on the second floor, looking out the window. The store had once been a house, and I was looking out the window and then I was in a house instead, as if I could turn around and see the bed—how fascinated I was with old beds, with the hollows in mattresses where the bodies had been. There it was, in the end, the slight shapes we left. A bed under the eaves, then looking out the window, then Nigel! How comfortable he seems in places he's never been before.

I pulled out a book and sat on a chair, on a mint-green leather chair, how unlike the green chair in my office, or the plastic sea-foam green chairs in the hospital. How magical green chairs always seemed to me. How magical the layers of meaning, though I've learned this is a way of dealing with the horror of non-being, this layering of time is a symptom of extreme states of anxiety. I sat in green chairs thinking these things and this was not something one could say: *Today I sat in green chairs and could feel where the bodies had been, where they had leaned.* I had gotten into trouble saying these things; there was no denying the look in someone's eyes when you said it.

After my breakdown they worried I would get ahead of myself, and there was no denying the problem that occurred when that happened. They said I was supposed to think about my toes, about the flow of blood to my toes, how squarely I rested on solid ground, but what I liked to do was think about lying on a blue comforter in a blue room, as if I was floating on the ocean and thinking there was no difference between lying on a blue comforter and lying on the ocean, as if there was a transporter in blue rooms. And then there was the problem. I was ahead of myself again, and there was no denying the problems that occurred when that happened. Nigel would say we have to get you thinking about something else. His favorite thing was to get me thinking about anthologies, and I did love anthologies, I did love broad cataloguing. He brought back catalogues from an antique auction, he gave me a whole box, he got me the whole back inventory... Here you go, Nora! That should keep you busy.

This passion for miniatures had brought me to a town of miniatures, a hamlet tucked inside a curve of the Hudson River, with tiny houses tumbled on top of tiny houses. My office was a small room that had been attached to a building like a lean-to. This building was in a maze of buildings, and the others surrounded it so completely that it was impossible to see my room from the outside. It was as if my room didn't exist except when I was inside of it. Perhaps, sensing space, spare footage, a previous landlord had attached the room, or perhaps it was a shed altered to pass for an office. I was not even certain that the people in the other offices knew about my office, though they seemed to understand that I came, went somewhere, emerged after a time.

In the room was a desk, a bookshelf, a green velvet chair, and dying African violets. I was sitting in the chair, *The Anthology of Small Homes* on my lap, when a fire alarm sounded, and we all issued out, eyes blinking in the sun. I wore a baggy polyester red coat. A large man in one of the upstairs offices had a cat, and he was particularly dainty with the cat, though not dainty otherwise. Damn fire alarm, he said, and with nothing better to do, I stood next to him in my coat and stretchy dark-wash jeans that had shrunk in the dryer. They circled above my ankles, displaying a shock of white athletic sock and my bird legs. I was petrified by the noise, and my hand was shaking inside my sleeve. They didn't notice, all the women talking in groups—I found it comforting how few people noticed anything. After a time the fire truck pulled in and we stood to the side, blinking, until they told us to go back in again.

Back in my green chair, with the book on my lap and hands still trembling, I flipped through the pages, just starting to relax when I reached a photograph of something called the Transcendent House. I didn't know the house, but something in it attracted my attention. It looked like a compilation of packing boxes stuck together helter-skelter. Each of the boxes was made of a different material; one blonde shingles, another corrugated metal, another wood that had been painted red. Everything—the windows, the door, the upstairs porch, even the chimney—was in perfect half-scale. Underneath was the sentence: *The Transcendent House was an art installation built on a farm in the Hudson Valley in 1972 by Wesley Lansing, a Brooklyn artist with a background in architecture.*

There was another photograph inset in the bottom corner, a black and white picture of the artist at the construction site. Behind him, sitting on the front steps of the house, was Nigel. Nigel as he would have looked thirty years ago. His face not so worn, not so faraway. He was speaking, gesturing with his hands. A young woman sat next to him. He commanded so much attention that I overlooked her at first. She was small, sitting with her legs bunched. She had on a baggy coat and skinny dark jeans. Her hair was my length. She was my age. She looked just like me. I didn't know what she was doing there, though she seemed to know. She was in conversation with Nigel. She was about to say something.

From my desk drawer, I took out a photograph of myself as a child. In it, I'm kneeling in a garden, pea tendrils around my hand. I'm looking at the camera and about to smile. Behind me is a chain-link fence with wild grass, and beyond that the ocean. My father left home when I was a little girl and I can't remember him, but I sensed him in the picture. There was something in my eyes, as if we had been gardening together and he had just disappeared and I hadn't realized it yet, and once I realized it, everything would change. My salt-dried hair in a halo of sun, my scraggly sundress with ribbon straps, the freckles on my shoulders, the peapod tendrils…

Research about the Transcendent House told me little. The newspaper articles all gave the same information. In 1971, a New York museum commissioned Wesley Lansing to build five houses in a field overlooking the Catskills. The museum accused Wesley of doing little of the work and pulled the funding after a year. They claimed the people building it were friends of his involved in anarchist activities. Lawsuits were threatened but never filed. According to records, none of the houses were ever built. I learned that Wesley had gone on to a successful career as a painter, and had an estate a few towns from where I lived, but I went there only to find it empty.

A curator at the museum searched for blueprints in the archives, but couldn't find them. She couldn't find a list of who had worked on the project, where the construction had been, could find no records of any kind. She was hurried on the phone, professional but not sympathetic. *Nothing?* I asked. *Not even something very little, anything, really?* No, she said, I couldn't find anything.

Nigel lived north along the river, in Hudson. Across the street from his apartment was a café with a black-and-white tiled floor and tin ceilings, and fake flowers on the tables. *A small coffee,* I said at the counter. Room for cream, someone asked. *Yes, just a little, I think, room for cream.*

I crossed and climbed the stairs to Nigel's apartment. He had a root beverage on his stove to replace his pot of coffee. He had digestive biscuits on an unfolded napkin and I sat captivated by the expanse of the napkin and the transparent splotches the biscuits left. Then, for a time, we argued. What is it? he asked. Your cookies? I forgot your cookies. *I'll be okay.* I'll run across the street. *I'm not eating those.* Try a biscuit. *I'm not eating those either.*

He wore a hunter green and navy flannel, threadbare at the elbows, the fabric so thin it rolled. One kitchen chair had a braided cushion, and I sat there while he sat on a wooden chair. I explained my progress on *Eminent Mariners: A Compilation of Famous Voyages and the Men Who Made Them.* Nigel's press was entirely composed of our pet projects, my great fondness for compilations of New England nautical history and his leaning towards the esoteric, the avantgarde, the necessity that nothing at all make sense. He was working on a set of anarchist pamphlets with silk-screened covers, and I was certain that he'd selected the texts because they matched the covers. Who was to say he'd ever read them? I never had, though we had spent countless hours poring over the minutia of their production.

He went to the floor and sifted through packets of paper samples, then scattered books all around, while I pondered the meaning of "a nascent New England mythology." Having at last acquired the final chapters of the book, I had sent it to be blurbed and was considering the responses. *I'm not certain if nascent New England mythology is a good thing*, I said. I looked under the table. Nigel was affixing new bookplates, patiently removing the old ones with a razor blade.

Have you thought about the book launch? he asked. What food we're going to serve?

I think the author is on a boat again.

Perhaps such matters should be figured out before we enter into contracts, don't you think? That might be essential in the future?

I asked him what he knew about the Transcendent House. I've thought of researching it for a book, I said.

He pulled off a bookplate and released it on the pile. The plates were curled and rustled like scattered leaves. Several times he ran a hand over them. Not very much, he said, what do you know?

Little, I said. I found it interesting, an article I read. Your name was mentioned.

That was a long time ago, he said. I was friends with the artist. I helped out at the site.

I thought you could tell me about it, anything you remember.

You don't know anything about it?

I think one house was built.

Yes, he said, one was built.

We talked quietly, and then he said, I find it hard to believe you haven't learned more. *No, nothing more.* There is a sense, then? *Some sense, but it's slight.* Ah, he said, your investigations, let's see if I can help, what I can do, but don't get your hopes up, I don't remember much from that time, and I don't know where the house is, if that's what you want, then I can't help. I went away and when I came back, the house was gone. They wouldn't tell me where it went. *Anything, really, is okay.* All right, then, he said.

I followed him to the bathroom where he kept a filing cabinet and more boxes. I sat on the lip of the porcelain tub, my hands under my butt to support my weight, while he dug through files. He kept finding things to exclaim over—A letter from Henry Miller! What a strange time in one's life, phone bills, did I ever even live there?, look, a receipt for a coffee carafe, I had forgotten all about that, and then here something is, years of looking and here it is when I wasn't even looking for it.

We started talking about work I might do once the nautical anthology was finished. *I wish I could do small houses,* I said. Yes, he said, we could just pretend we didn't know it had been done already, or perhaps true miniatures—there are these dollhouses with exact replicas of Victorian furniture. There's something to fascinate you. They have whole auctions of those things. God, I don't know why I keep the things I keep, and get rid of precisely the things I shouldn't. He slid the file drawer closed, thought to restack the boxes, but stayed crouched on the floor, looking at me. Something stilled when he looked at me. I slid the younger version of him over this one. The years had not been gentle, yes, there had been damage. You could see that now.

His lips moved as if about to tell me something, but I must have started to bite my lip. It wasn't because my hands were moving—I was sitting on my hands—but the moment of stillness was ruffled, he was all movement again, poking at boxes, talking too quickly. There was a file, he said, with blueprints and photographs, but I can't find it. Who knows why I am the way I am. It seems exactly the thing I shouldn't have lost, but where could I have put it?

Weeks later he decided I might do a barn anthology. *I thought I was doing miniatures,* I said. I was on the floor of his kitchen, typing a press release. *I'd prefer miniatures.* I looked into it, he said, and dollhouses have been done, too. *Barns, surely, have been done.* But not in this way. *What way are we doing barns?* It's all loose in my mind right now, ephemeral, floating. *I'd still prefer miniatures.* Perhaps it's time to expand your interests. *I don't think barns, though.*

The next day we went looking for barns—him sitting in the passenger seat, me driving, light pooling across our faces, his head rolled to look out the window, the back seat of the car lined with maps. Look at that one, he kept saying, clicking a fingernail on the window as if he could touch it. We passed many barns, until we got to one and he told me to pull over. It was the silver gray color he liked, and it was off in the distance, on a slope, the isolation he liked, and this had not been unusual, for us to stop, look at something. *Okay?* I said, but he wanted to get out. *No, there's a house, they'll see us.* What will they think we're doing, stealing the barn? *I don't know, it will look strange.* He got out and lumbered up the slope. I sat with my hands on the steering wheel. Finally, I followed him. Okay, he said, stand here. Now walk and look at the barn. Afterward he asked, Did you see it? *It?* The light?

It would be easier if you told me what I'm looking for, I said. I stood in the mud, arms at my side, the sky suddenly very high, alarmingly high (no, I didn't have agoraphobia, but what did I have then, if not agoraphobia?—it was just everything was so high, so out of scale with our being. It's okay, Nora! he would usually say if he noticed my hands flutter, which they had begun to do; it's time then, back to the car, let's talk about catalogues!, but he kept looking at me as if trying to figure something out). He stood away from me, not moving, in a patch of gold grass that was moving in the wind. He wore a tan field coat that reached his thighs and billowed open, showing a hunter-green lining. His rubber boots were tan with green laces. I told him, the grass matches your outfit. Everything around you is moving, your coat is moving, but you're not moving.

Okay, he said. I want to show you this.

We walked together. I went up to his shoulders and seemed to flit there. He motioned, pointing out the lines of light between each plank, showing me how the light came through from the other side so that when we walked, it seemed as if we were staying still and the light was moving, the splinter between each plank moving as if on rails, the tick-tick of movement… I can't say what it makes me feel, he said. The light moving as if the building is sparkling, the stripped silver gray; it's like there's something inside it, as if the light is coming from inside. It's hard to say precisely what it is, the negative space, something in how it's alone in a field; though, of course, there are different kinds of barns, but I think it's this kind where they put the house, a building inside a building, and I can't get to it… He trailed off, but kept looking at the barn, as if trying to extract something from it.

What he meant by this I couldn't be sure. Something about the Transcendent House. He thought it was hidden in a barn. For a long time he had been searching barns, but he no longer believed he could find it. My hands were cold and I had forgotten gloves. He kept trying to say what he meant, but then people came out of the house, two people, a father and daughter, and they watched us. Why are they watching us? I asked. They look like us, I said, why do they look like us? We stood at the top of the hill and they stood at the bottom, two figures, one tall and one small, watching us, as if we were looking in a mirror. I wanted to go back to the car but Nigel kept trying to tell me something. There is something in the emptiness of the space, empty but not empty, you can see through it but there's something in that space… I don't know anymore, after all this time, if I were to find the barn, if the house would still be inside. It has become impossible to find, everywhere and nowhere at once… His eyes, the eeriness of them, the translucent orbs looking off at the distance, later I would watch him stacking books on his kitchen floor, tan linoleum with brown patterns, green shades over the windows, he had been gone often at the doctor's during this time, and I would try to interest him in the books. No, no, he would say when I asked him if it could be an anthology, an anthology of photographs of barns? Or, I would say, not in a literal sense but as an abstraction, barn abstractions—even for us, an anthologization of abstract notions of a barn, isn't that a little much? He said, I couldn't find the house when I came back, and I said, *Where did you go?* He didn't answer, so I said, *I've decided that nascent New England mythology is a good thing.* And he thought for a moment, and then said, Yes, I think so. I think you are right.

For a long time after he died, I didn't know what had happened to his things. No one told me. I sat in the coffee shop across the street from his apartment. I crossed and climbed the stairs. Everything had been swept except for a scattering of pine needles.

When I learned his family had donated his belongings to the library of a private college in Maine, I drove up. I hadn't known much about his life, hadn't known that he had been raised along the coast of Maine by an abusive father, that he had reached some renown in his early twenties with found poetry and mail art, that he was married with a young daughter but had left his wife and daughter and suffered a nervous breakdown, alone, in a shack in the Philippines, some time after the Transcendent House had been built.

I pieced this together in the college's archives, through letters, articles, journals, an account a friend had written about a group of them in Maine; they'd slept on mattresses from the dump and littered the front yard with found-object sculptures. Nigel slept in the garage, under blankets wet from a leaky roof. During the day, they sat on benches outside the library, frightening and fascinating residents who gave them food and objects for the sculptures—

used pie tins, car parts. I sat at a long wooden table, with a pencil stub and squares of scrap paper as if I was going to take notes. Light moved across the room. I moved to an upholstered chair in the corner.

Later, I wandered the stacks. They had added Nigel's books to the main collection, and I found them, those tiny paperbacks, always the cheapest editions, the sort that used to be in airport carrels, a sensationalized picture on the cover, the edges brick red. I kept pulling a book out, finding the bookplate, then putting it back. Many times I did this, then the librarian came over, You forgot your bag, she said, and handed it to me but stayed there. *I do that, sometimes*, I said, *forget my bag, it's never quite where I need it.* Yes, she said, sometimes I leave mine, too.

Library shelves sometimes seemed impossibly high to me, towering, and that was how they seemed then.

Wesley Lansing owned an estate called Grove Hill a few towns south of me. The estate was hidden along a dirt road that sloped to the river. I found him at the post office and followed him from a distance. He walked to his studio. It was in a partially converted carriage house below the estate, with a wall of floor-to-ceiling windows that overlooked the river. Huge canvases of colored lines hung on the walls.

In the afternoon, the wall of windows was a still liquid that diffused light and shadows, but as it grew dark, the room lit like a jewel. Wesley lay down on a black leather chaise in the corner of the room. I stood in the snow and watched him. I had also watched him at the restaurant of the local hotel, where he hosted a group of friends from the city. He went on about the food. I sat at the bar, my legs dangling above the footrest. One must have pot roast when in the country! he exclaimed. There was a mirror over the bar, and I could see him in the mirror. He bought everyone a round of bourbon, but ordered coffee for himself. It was storming outside, and the lights flickered above the bar. Everyone at the table laughed, their soft faces, their soft candle-lit hair thrown back.

While sleeping, Wesley looked older and sad. He looked as if something had been taken away from him. After a time, as if I had been planning it, though I didn't know what I was doing until my hand was on the knob, I entered the studio and walked to a door on the other side. It opened into the dark unconverted part of the carriage house. Inside, by the light from the studio, I saw another door. I walked ahead, opened it, went back, closed the studio door, and groped in the darkness for the entrance.

Afterwards, I had to work to recall what happened. By trying to remember if it was a pleasant memory or an unpleasant one, I found it both warm and sad. Then I remembered Nigel's face, so close I could have touched it.

We were sitting on the front steps. People were milling around, packing up. They were letting us be, giving us a chance to say goodbye. Nigel's face was round, his skin white and soft. His eyes were brighter. He was talking quickly, there was something agitated, something not right with him. The work on the house was over. The funding had been pulled. He needed to get away. He was going to work at an English-language newspaper in the Philippines. He was only going for a brief time. He would come back. He told me all this, then his voice grew gentler. What is it, Nora? he said.

I shook my head, wisps of hair catching in my mouth. I sat with my knees together, my body hunched, and could see in his eyes what I looked like: on the verge of saying something, but unable.

He said, It's okay if you can't say it, and then he wasn't there. I went into the house only to find the pegs on the wall empty. His scarf gone, his coat. My mother was packing. She was wrapping dishes in old newspaper. The beige ceramic would hold black smudges when we unpacked later. She would remove the smudges by licking her thumb, then wiping each dish as if it had done something to her. She wanted me outside, in the garden. But I went up to my room. None of my things were there. My bed was gone. When I went into their room, it was empty. She called for me in the garden, then went down the path to the ocean. She called my name, then stopped calling. Neighbors had come to load the boxes. No one noticed me downstairs. No one noticed that through the open door you couldn't see anything; it was like the brightest sun. They were walking with boxes into it, and they were so high, and the boxes so large, they didn't notice a slight figure brushing through the frame.

I spilled back into Wesley's studio. He was awake, watching me, ripped from security at the sight of me. Did he remember, too? Was the sight of me all this time a ghost memory? Or had he remembered nothing? I thought all this as I walked from the studio, not turning to close the door, wandering down the hill—sneakers wet with snow, red coat snagging in briars—aware, only later, that it had begun to snow, as in the distance I heard the train, saw the glow of the lighthouse along the river.

THE BOOK OF

Christian Hawkey

the book of dip netting beaks, the book of
mud probing beaks, the book of kissing
as a form of knife sharpening,
the book of lovers & the book of beloveds,
the book of glass, float glass,
& the book of bodies, bodies as birds
slamming into glass, into invisible things, the idea
of invisible things, the book of religion
& the book of the dead, the half dead,
the newly dead, the almost dead, the nearly dead,
those dead as door nails, dead as a dead phrase,
& the book of the resuscitated, the reanimated,
the book of flesh sewn together, organs harvested,
blood transfused, the book of zombies
& the book of consciousness,
the book of consciousness tucked under the rotting arm
of a zombie stumbling sunward,
lightward, humanward, the 9th ward,
the flooded ward, the ward of humans
as numbers, any number of humans
reading the book of happiness,
the book of pills, the book of oracles & auricles
& the book of homophones & heteronyms,
sand-filled orifices, light-filled orifices,
pain-filled, toy-filled, vegetable-filled,
word-filled, or used to speak words,
the book of or, of of, of b, of beginnings
& of books that also begin, that end

or never end, the coverless book, the pageless book,
the book of waterfalls, the book of scrolls,
the scroll of the book of waterfalls & the one
reading there, falling there, surfacing
in the book of noise, spells, spellings,
one for each one, one for every image
circulating, unbound, holding
the image of a book in hand, the image of
a face in hand, a face from the book of faces,
fleshless, odorless, a face the size of a
thumbnail, compressed, encoded,
a series of numbers, immaterial, a face
in a river of faces, streaming, where are you
now, where is your head now, your face now

THE HABIT OF VOYAGING

Adam Gopnik & Jean-Marie Gustave Le Clézio

ADAM GOPNIK: I was going to welcome you to America, but of course you need no welcoming to America. You've come to us tonight from that French outpost of Albuquerque, New Mexico.

JEAN-MARIE GUSTAVE LE CLÉZIO: Yes, this is true. I have been living for more than ten years in New Mexico. I'm more New Mexican than anything else.

GOPNIK: What was it that lured you to Albuquerque?

LE CLÉZIO: I was teaching in a small college in the central part of Mexico, in Michoacán, and the situation there got rather bad—for people with small children it became kind of dangerous. So my wife and I decided to move, and we did like most people in Mexico: We crossed the border. And on the other side was New Mexico. So we settled there and I began teaching at the University of New Mexico, after having taught in Michoacán.

GOPNIK: You know America extraordinarily well. You've been not just *in* America, but all over America.

LE CLÉZIO: I've traveled quite a lot in the U.S., and also in Latin America. I like very much the "New World." To me, it's appealing.

GOPNIK: One of the things that's distinctive in your work is exactly its geographic range—the habit of travel, the habit of voyaging. But as I've read about you, that isn't something that you acquired later on. It's, in some ways, in your DNA. It was your natural language as a child.

This transcript was adapted from a public conversation held at the 2009 PEN World Voices Festival of International Literature.

LE CLÉZIO: I'm a Breton, from Brittany. And the Bretons were very poor, like the Irish. So whenever they could, they left Brittany to find a better world. My ancestors left Brittany and went to Mauritius. And Mauritius is a very small island, so very soon they had to leave there, too. My father was a medical officer, first in British Guiana, and then in Nigeria. One of my uncles was a doctor in Trinidad, another was in Réunion Island. Some of my aunts went to live in South Africa. I think we are nearly everywhere.

GOPNIK: On your father's side, English speakers?

LE CLÉZIO: Not really English speakers because in Mauritius you speak French, English, and Creole. So their real language was Creole. Then they took on French and they took on English. English was for scientific matters at school, French was more for literary things, and Creole was for general life.

GOPNIK: So that idea of a Creolized society, where there is no one authentic language or one true culture, is essential to you?

LE CLÉZIO: Yes, I strongly believe that Creolization is a good thing. You have to mix and you have to change your identity and adapt to a new way of life, especially when you travel. The lesson I received from my parents was that we have to adapt, we have to find new places and a new way of life. My mother went back to France at the beginning of the war to see her family, while my father was in Nigeria. So I was brought up in the south of France. But I always thought that I did not belong really to that place, that one day I would probably go to Mauritius, or some other place. And when my father retired from the British military he looked for a warm place to live. He was thinking Bermuda or the Bahamas or Malta. For some reason he didn't want to go back to Mauritius; maybe he had some problems there. Eventually he settled in Nice, which was warm enough for him.

GOPNIK: You ended up being there through the Second World War as a young boy.

LE CLÉZIO: Yes. It was strange to realize one day that all my early childhood took place during war. One of my early memories is a bomb falling very close to my grandmother's home where we were living. The ground was shaking. This bomb was dropped by Canadians, because there were Germans in Nice, and—

GOPNIK: Canadians, really?

LE CLÉZIO: Yeah, Canadians.

GOPNIK: We apologize.

LE CLÉZIO: It was for a good reason: to get rid of the Germans. But still, I remember the noise. I remember falling on the ground and shrieking. So when I think about wars it's a personal experience. It's not something I read about in books.

GOPNIK: It returns as a theme in so much of your writing—the experience of children in war, as in *Wandering Star*.

LE CLÉZIO: Yes, well, I can't rely on historical knowledge when I write. I read books afterwards, to learn more, but my first knowledge is always personal, made of feelings, sensations. I remember having been very hungry, and I remember being on the road and seeing Americans approaching, and begging for food. Like sometimes you see those images in the newspaper—in Darfur, for example. Soldiers passing by and children begging for food. I begged for food. And they threw me some chewing gum, some very good white bread, made from a very enriched flour, this very white type of flour.

GOPNIK: Wonder Bread.

LE CLÉZIO: Exactly. And a box of Spam. And those three things for me were the beginning of life. I had been eating rutabagas, you know those rotten roots? Suddenly I met real food. Spam was real food.

GOPNIK: That's a great moment in Franco-American relations. We sent Spam and Wonder Bread, they gave us back Le Clézio. One of the things that makes your work so arresting and original is the combination of this extraordinarily cosmopolitan point of view with the extraordinary purity and beauty of your French. French language is another country for you. It's a place you've lived your whole life.

LE CLÉZIO: Being from Mauritius, I couldn't call any place my country. France was a country where I was living, but it was not my country. My country was in the imagination, and it was difficult to explain to my fellow students, my comrades, to say, "I am from Mauritius." They would not know at that time what Mauritius was. They would say, "Oh yes, St-Maurice? Where would that be?" St-Maurice was a part of Nice. "No," I would say, "It's a bit farther. It's not that close." I could not explain to what I really belonged.

So I had to find a place where I would belong, where I would find myself. And this place was books. Fortunately my grandmother and my grandfather had a very good library. They had a good collection of books, and I read French, Spanish, English literature. When I was a child there were no books for children, so I read *Don Quixote* when I was a child like it was a book meant for children. *Lazarillo de Tormes*, *The Ingoldsby Legends*—those were my first books. And I felt that language was my real place, and I began to write. I began to feel I could pertain to this world of books. I was a lover of books—and especially of dictionaries. I really enjoy going through dictionaries.

GOPNIK: Just reading a dictionary as a novel?

LE CLÉZIO: Yes, yes. The French dictionary—and there was the *Encyclopædia Britannica*, which is a marvelous source of knowledge.

GOPNIK: The illustrated *Larousse* dictionary, that's such a beautiful—

LE CLÉZIO: Yes, it's very beautiful. It's amazing because I still see life through those pages, the definitions of that time. There was an extraordinary collection of dictionaries called *Dictionnaire de la conversation*, "conversation dictionaries," which were meant for young women of the nineteenth century, so that they would not humiliate their husbands.

GOPNIK: Polite conversation that they could—

LE CLÉZIO: Polite conversation, and good knowledge on historical matters. Because women could not go to school in the nineteenth century, so it was one way of being educated. I read those books, and I have a strange perception of the world from those articles.

GOPNIK: That makes me think about your early work especially—one of the striking things about it is its extreme precision. May I read a favorite quote of yours, if you'll forgive me, in my own bad translation?

LE CLÉZIO: Please do.

GOPNIK: You wrote, in 1967, I think: "I am a lover of details. I love all that is small. I have respect for animals and for objects. The closer they can be held, the more they please me. We all have an imprecise image of life. Mine is made of small details. A room, for instance, with a warm rug, a flower, cigarette ashes in an ashtray." And then you go on to describe beautifully the contents of a single room, and you end by saying, "In my room, in the street, the city, on all the earth, and even elsewhere, there are many small gods. And I prostrate myself before each of them." Was that a kind of credo of your work early on?

LE CLÉZIO: For a long time I thought that writing would be a kind of enumeration of things and of words. One of the first modern authors I read was Jerome David Salinger. I heard that he used to go to a small hut in his backyard and write words on paper. He would make an enumeration. And I said to myself, "This is writing. This is a good writer. I should do the same." So I was trying to imitate Salinger in enumerating things, enumerating words, and then choosing them and using them—because each word is a world by itself. It opens onto a scenario, a story, a legend, or a myth. Every word contains a world.

GOPNIK: Nicely said. I wanted to ask you about Salinger because I've noticed in your comments on your own work Salinger came up very early for you. And, of course, he's one of the local gods at *The New Yorker*, where I work. What was it about Salinger? The idea of enumerating words, to start—but would we be wrong to think also the ability to inhabit the mind of an adolescent, as in *The Catcher in the Rye*?

LE CLÉZIO: Yes. And he taught me that there might be a confrontation between power, the power that comes from writing, and the inner self that expresses literature.

GOPNIK: The soul of literature against the show of literature.

LE CLÉZIO: Yes. Power to Salinger meant something static, while the inner self, the soul, meant something that was difficult to define, something moving all the time, not steady.

GOPNIK: Your work has been a series of escapes, in a sense, in an effort to stay close to the soul of literature and away from the power of literature.

LE CLÉZIO: Yes, to have this evasive perception of the world, full of details, but incapable of reaching a point where you say, "I know something." You never know something. Literature is the contrary of knowledge—it's asking questions. It's the contrary of affirmation.

GOPNIK: Or having a message.

LE CLÉZIO: Yes. During that time, after the Second World War, people were not sure of anything. The world had crumbled, literally, especially in Europe. When I was, say, ten to fifteen years old, we were sure of absolutely nothing. And at the end of this period came another terrible war, the Algerian War, for which I was drafted. Those were terrible times. After that you could not believe in commitment in literature. Literature could not give lessons. Literature could only question and express your angst, your anger, and sometimes your derision—but it could not give you security.

GOPNIK: In a way the first fifteen to twenty years of your work is a negation of the littérature engagée of Malraux and similar thinkers.

LE CLÉZIO: Not that I didn't like it. I enjoyed reading *La Condition humaine*, and reading *Huis clos* and other plays by Sartre. But in some ways those authors failed. I don't know why. Maybe my generation failed, or maybe—

GOPNIK: All generations fail, perhaps.

LE CLÉZIO: Maybe. And in our case the failure was the Algerian War. After the Second World War, in France especially, the Algerian War was the most terrible thing that could have happened, because people were trying to impose themselves on another nation, to be a colonial power. This is impossible to admit to oneself. So I wanted to leave France. I wanted to live in Sweden or England, or Canada maybe, because those places were far from this colonial war.

GOPNIK: And yet I've always imagined a kind of subterranean, clandestine dialogue between you and Camus. Do you feel that at all?

LE CLÉZIO: I liked Camus because he did not give affirmations. Even in his Nobel Prize speech he said he could not choose between Algerian independence and the love he had for his native land and for his mother. He showed a kind of weakness, and for this I loved him. He was convinced that the world had no other meaning but the meaning we could give, what we could want the world to be. So that apparent contradiction I appreciated in Camus.

GOPNIK: It's a theme of your work, too, it seems to me: the contradictions of experience, contradictions of consciousness. You never resolve anything in simplicity.

LE CLÉZIO: There was another link: Like Camus, I spent most of my childhood on the Mediterranean. I was just on the other side of that sea. Some of my friends at school were killed in Algeria. As soon as they arrived there they were killed. So I had the feeling that I was very close to this amazingly sharp world with strong light, beautiful scenery, the sea—and all this was the background to angst and the fear of war. This, I think, was an important part of my education. When I tried to read the Greek philosophers, I found they gave me the same angst, the same questions about being. "What is being?" It's a sunny country, so you should not normally ask those questions. But still it's there, and very strongly. There is an angst in Parmenides. The pre-Socratic philosophers are full of angst, full of questions.

GOPNIK: It's part of the landscape of that world.

LE CLÉZIO: In a vain way, I thought myself very lucky to have grown up in such scenery. Because reading those texts, reading about Camus, and doing that outside in the shade of an olive tree, I felt that it was a kind of privilege.

GOPNIK: Landscape plays a hugely important role in all of your writing, doesn't it?

LE CLÉZIO: Yes. I was a strong believer in writing outside, "en plein air," at the beach, even. We would take books to the beach and read in the sun, and I felt a connection between the sun and feeling the strength of nature. This was also a privilege. I could not do that in Paris or in London.

GOPNIK: In much of your work, you intermingle human consciousness with animal consciousness, with the simple existence of the inarticulate world, so that you always have a simultaneous sense not only of the human mind, but also of the permanent existence of the planet.

LE CLÉZIO: I don't feel that human beings are very different from the rest of creation. We all partake of this world. And we share everything in that world. We have the same passions and the same instincts, sometimes even the same language and the same dreams as the animals—and probably the vegetation. The novel is a pleasant form for writing because you can fill the novel with all these different passions. You tell a story, you invent people, you make them talk—but at the same time you see them in their surroundings. You can see how they are surrounded by plants, by trees. You can even conceive that towns are part of nature, that they are a production of nature—that everything is connected. That's why I like writing novels.

GOPNIK: A reader of yours said that one of your ambitions, if one had to describe it in a phrase, would be "a humanism without human beings at the center." That is, the values of humanism without the notion of the human being as the sole controller and consciousness of the world.

LE CLÉZIO: I wish I could do that, but I am a human being, so everything I do is from a human point of view. But I like to imagine, sometimes. And there are many books in which you can find this moving and troubling sense of something which is not entirely human. You find that in ancient books, like the Mahabharata, an extraordinary book where the forest has such a role in the story. The forest surrounds the heroes, and it acts, and it has a philosophical meaning in the story of humanity. Or in some poems—Rimbaud's, for instance—you can feel the impulse coming from the light, from the sun. Rimbaud says in one of his poems that what he likes is to roam in dirty streets and suddenly feel the sun on his face, and he calls the sun the god of fire. And this, for me—it's astonishing. When I read this it makes me shiver.

GOPNIK: Some say that your first books—for example, *The Interrogation*, as it's called in English translation—are related to the movement called "the new novel" in France, but that as you went on there was a break in your work where you became less aggressively experimental and more accessible. Do you see that as a break, or do you see it as an evolution of a single project?

LE CLÉZIO: It's probably both. When I published *The Interrogation* I was in France. I was twenty-two years old. When you are twenty-two you want to break doors, you want to be violent, to say that you exist. "I am here. I exist. And I want to say something." But then the years pass by, you have good and bad experiences, and you change. You begin to understand that your aim is not necessarily to say, "I exist," but to try to be the vector or the passage for something else, something you perceive and want to transmit. That's probably the reason I was less aggressive after my early books.

But I never felt I was linked to the nouveau roman. When I sent my first book to the publisher it was together with a letter addressed to the editor saying, "This is not a 'new novel.'" I wanted to make a strong separation. At that time I felt more linked to the so-called New York Jewish novel—Salinger, for example. I felt more attracted by those writers because they spoke about rebellion, and I didn't find that in the nouveau roman, which was just a reaction against commitment literature, against the previous generation, which followed the war. The only novel I really appreciated was a novel by Nathalie Sarraute, called *L'Ère du soupçon*—*The Era of*... How do you say "soupçon"?

GOPNIK: Suspicion or mistrust.

LE CLÉZIO: The era of mistrust, of suspicion. This was what I felt. I felt a strong suspicion of the previous French literature—and even of Steinbeck, that type of literature.

GOPNIK: Of Hemingway?

LE CLÉZIO: Especially Hemingway, yes.

GOPNIK: Literature that wanted to conquer the world.

LE CLÉZIO: And to deliver a message to the world. To say, "These are the solutions." This was the same moment when, for instance, the socialists in Russia and China were committing great crimes, and the interrogators of that time were denying the crimes. I remember people going to China and they never saw what was happening there. I don't know—they were blind to it, perhaps.

GOPNIK: Or chose not to see.

LE CLÉZIO: The "era of suspicion" is a good definition for that period.

GOPNIK: And yet, as the decades have gone on, in France at least, you're perceived as someone who has brought a kind of message, the message, if you like, of the existence of a world outside our world—the idea that the world is not defined by the narrow preoccupations of Paris or New York or the little nut of western civilization.

LE CLÉZIO: I felt very much that way because, in fact, I didn't live in Paris.

GOPNIK: You never lived in Paris until very recently.

LE CLÉZIO: I was reluctant. When I got the prize I was in Nice and my father said, "Take the train. Go to Paris. You have to go there." And I asked him, "What should I do in Paris? What should I see?" They were asking me for pictures, so I went to a photo booth and sent those pictures to the publisher.

GOPNIK: This is when you won the Prix Renaudot. So you went to one of those things where you got the strip of photographs?

LE CLÉZIO: Yes, that's what I sent. And I felt then the beginning of a new era in French literature, in which people belonging to former French colonies were taking on French to write their own stories. Paris was a village and the French language was extending itself to the entire world. *The Wretched of the Earth*, Frantz Fanon, for instance, and Édouard Glissant. Or Aimé Césaire, from Martinique, who wrote an extraordinary book of poetry called *Cahier d'un retour au pays natale—Notebook of a Return to the Native Land*. All those people writing about their experience of colonialism and their will to be free, their need to be free. One of the good writers of that time is Déwé Gorodé from New Caledonia, who was put in jail by the French because she was claiming independence for New Caledonia. She wrote good poetry, good novels, and a very interesting speech in which she says that the Kanak people from New Caledonia cannot be independent until they know how to treat women, because they have a very patriarchal way of life. All these people were giving new breath to French literature—a new space, a new future. This was really the new novel and the new poetry.

GOPNIK: This was the real nouveau roman.

LE CLÉZIO: Yes. The best writers in French literature now are from Africa and the West Indies, from Québec—like Rita Mestokosho, who writes beautiful poetry about trees, about the river, about the way she talks to the salmon, and who is fighting against the multinationals who want to build a dam on her river, the Romaine River. Those are the people who have something to say, and it's beautiful that they use the French language. If the French culture had the guilt of being a slave-trading and colonialist culture, now they are forgiven in some sense by the use of French for those different countries.

GOPNIK: Part of your life has been spent bearing witness to that new use of the language.

LE CLÉZIO: I was sensitive, I think, to the wrongs of colonization, because I went, as a child, to Africa, to Nigeria, to meet my father when he was working as a doctor there. This was during the colonization of Nigeria by the British. It was not better than the French colonization. It was terrible. I still remember violent images: African people working as a chain gang on the roads. They worked under the sun and were led to a place where they would build the swimming pool of the district officer. He was watching them, not moving, with his white helmet and his colonial clothes. When I read about the slave trade, I know what it means. I've seen scenes like those. My father was strongly against colonialism, though he belonged to the system. He was persuaded that it was wrong to be there in such a system. This is what I'm made of, those images and those teachings from my own family. Being from Mauritius, I come from a colonialist family—because in the past, the French people in Mauritius, they traded slaves and they imported from China and from India, the same way people did in the southern states of the U.S. All those things to me are connected. When I read Faulkner, I listen well to what he speaks about, because I've been, in certain ways, to the same culture. I have the same feeling of guilt and the same feeling of compassion and the same urge to see things change—to see the world be a true and just place, not a place of injustice as it still is now.

GOPNIK: It strikes me as we talk that it has absolute reality for you—that the history of colonialism and enslavement isn't something you can easily put off as being part of a remote past. For you, it's happening now. It weighs on you.

LE CLÉZIO: I think I am unable to write about things I have not seen or I have not been told about. If you told me something, then I could write about it. But I can't dare to imagine things—for instance, to write a historical novel. I could only dare to speak about the Jewish people living in Saint-Martin and trying to cross the Alps, to write about that, because my mother told me that story, which is not very well known. When I have seen something or I have been told something, that's the beginning of literature. Then it can be changed into a novel, into a legend, into a poem or into any literary shape.

GOPNIK: It has to be tangible, it has to be a particular story.

LE CLÉZIO: It has to be seen through the eyes, my eyes or your eyes. I have to have that real connection with the memory.

GOPNIK: One of your most beautiful novels, in my view, is called *Wandering Star*. In it, you tell the story of a Jewish girl at the creation of the state of Israel and the story of a Palestinian girl at the same time. It's a perfect example, it seems to me, of your desire to have a novel that bears witness, but bears no message.

LE CLÉZIO: It's linked also with my childhood in the back country of Nice. My mother, my grandmother, my grandfather, they had to flee from Nice because the Germans were coming. So we went into hiding in the mountains and we didn't know at the time that in the next village, about six miles from the place where we were, the Italians had gathered the Jewish people from the coast. Shortly after the war, my mother began to talk about that, and then when I was older, she told me the whole story. For me, it was extraordinary that I had been so close to this drama, and I wanted very much to write about that—because I felt I had been part of it in some way. I was there. Maybe I saw some of the children who were taken by the Germans and sent to the death camps. I felt I had to write about that—not because I felt I could do something about it, but because I wanted to free myself, in a certain way, of this terrible history, which was a grand history at the same time. I wanted to write a novel about this moment. My mother told me about what had happened after I had begun a short story about a Palestinian camp. I was thinking of publishing that separately, but for some reason I saw suddenly that the stories could be linked. I wrote the novel and then I asked myself, "Is it a caricature that I'm writing? Is it too similar?" I did not want to express the idea that the Palestinian people were living the same thing that the Jewish people had lived. I was reluctant to publish it. And this lasted for years, because at the moment I was writing that short story about the Palestinian camp, the first Intifada began. So I said, "I can't publish it now, because it would looks as if I was taking advantage of the situation, was making profit off of it." So I held onto it for some years and then slowly, I took it up again, and managed to write the book. But I suppressed a part of the book that took place in Lebanon.

GOPNIK: Because?

LE CLÉZIO: Because it was too close to actuality. I wanted it to be a novel, not a kind of pamphlet, or reportage. I wanted to keep the shape of a novel. It took me about four or five years to complete.

GOPNIK: And yet it does represent, quite beautifully, it seems to me, for lack of a better phrase, the common humanity of these two experiences.

LE CLÉZIO: For me, the motivation was to complete memory. I had received from my mother her memory so many years ago. I felt I had been a witness of what had happened in the south Alps in France and at the same time I felt I was a contemporary witness of what was happening in Palestine. And I wanted the memory and the extrapolation that came from my reading the paper. I'd never been to Israel or Palestine. The first time I went there I went through Jordan. I wanted to cross the river, but something happened and the border was closed. So I went back to Amman. I've never been there.

GOPNIK: Oh, really? Because the novel is a beautiful evocation of landscape and light.

LE CLÉZIO: I saw it from afar. I was on the cliff on the other side. I saw Jerusalem shining in the fog.

GOPNIK: That seems to be a pattern in your life, being just outside and seeing from the border. In your Nobel lecture you addressed the question of whether this new world that's coming into being—what everyone calls the south, or the third world, the dispossessed world—whether it can find a voice of its own that can not just contribute, but find its own autonomy. How do you see that development? And can literature generally play a role in the twenty-first century?

LE CLÉZIO: I believe strongly that literature is one of the ways to achieve interculturality. If we don't achieve it through words and through the imagination, then it will never be possible. It has to exist first in books and in the imagination. The fact that all cultures have a right to express themselves and that there is no culture better than the other—they are not alike, but they have a right to the general concert of the human spirit. Literature is a way to achieve this. It's a rare occasion of being able to hear the world voices—it's a beautiful phrase, "world voices." We have to listen to the world voices, and I think literature is a good way to do so, because novelists and poets are probably less concerned with power, less concerned with politics. Sometimes they suffer from politics, they suffer from censorship; they are jailed and even sometimes killed. But novelists have a freedom of mind, because they make their heroes with their words, and they give us a sort of play, a theatrical play, which is felt from the inside. When you read a novel, at a certain point you get inside, you are swallowed by the novel. When I read *The Catcher in the Rye* I am Holden Caulfield. At a certain point I am inside his head, his body. And being inside others, changing your personality, even, when you write, helps you to better understand others. It's a way of going towards the other, of understanding the other. If we read Déwé Gorodé, we can't deny that what she says about New Caledonia is right. I am a New Caledonian when I read her work. I strongly feel what she says, what she asks for. When I read Richard Wright, I feel that also. Each time I read a novel which enthralls me, I leave my personal identity and I begin to be the other. I think that is the key.

GOPNIK: Literature is our most powerful means to inhabit the other.

LE CLÉZIO: Exactly. It is the best way to understand and to begin to love the other, to be close to the other. I strongly believe all this is a matter of love. There is a beautiful poem by Francisco de Quevedo, who says that "Love is the only real dimension of the world." And I think literature is made of that.

Even when you read a terrible novel, it was made with a compassion or love for humanity. You can't deny it. It exists. Even the worst situations express this concern for the other.

GOPNIK: We wouldn't write at all if we didn't feel that.

LE CLÉZIO: Of course. I am sure that *Frankenstein* by Mary Shelley expresses something real, a real experience which she lived through. It expresses the preoccupation that there is a monster in us also—and knowing that we can be monsters helps us to cure ourselves.

GOPNIK: Speaking of the others, let us inhabit some of them if we can. I know some in the audience have questions, and I know Mr. Le Clézio would be delighted to take them.

AUDIENCE: You talk about landscape so much, and I wonder, how would you describe the landscape of your mind? And what novels are you reading now?

LE CLÉZIO: I'll answer the second question first: I'm reading *The Interesting Narrative of the Life of Olaudah Equiano*, a marvelous book written in 1750 by an African who was taken from the Niger River and sold as a slave in the United States. Then he went with a captain and visited the Arctic Pole and then he went to Europe and then back to the United States. He traveled a lot, and learned a lot about himself. I'm reading it because he had a sister—I don't know if it's a twin sister, but he mentions a sister, taken at the same time as himself, and we never knew what happened to her. So it's a book with a blank half.

GOPNIK: Sounds like the beginning of a novel.

LE CLÉZIO: Could be. But it's fascinating. It's not a novel, really, it's a diary. It was also essential to the abolitionist movement in the United States. This is what I am reading now. And as to the other question, the landscape in my mind—I must say, I am very much attracted to the North Pole. I would like very much to be there sometimes. I have a vision of a totally icy world without any plants.

GOPNIK: Have you ever traveled to the Arctic?

LE CLÉZIO: Never.

GOPNIK: On behalf of Canada, I would like you to go see it.

LE CLÉZIO: It's one of my dreams. I probably will never do it, but some of my nights are filled with icy landscapes shining under a very blue sky with a very strong sun.

GOPNIK: We must get you north.

AUDIENCE: Before the Nobel Committee awarded you the prize, they made some remarks about American readers and their seeming lack of interest in current world literature. I wondered if you had any comments about that.

GOPNIK: Let me turn that question around, if the gentleman doesn't mind. Instead of asking about any imagined insult to America, let me ask about a compliment to France. Your winning the Nobel Prize seemed to be, if not a vindication, at least a reaffirmation of the importance of French literature at a moment when many people have said that French literature no longer matters as it once did.

LE CLÉZIO: Yes, I understand that notion. Unfortunately, I am Mauritian as well as French. I have two nationalities, two passports. I belong to both nations. And furthermore, I don't think that literature has to be strictly connected to a nation, to a nationality. Literature is making use of language. Joseph Conrad, for instance, wrote in English, but he was not an Englishman. Samuel Beckett wrote in French; he was Irish. So you don't belong to a nationality, you belong to the language in which you write. For me, French is not a declining language at all. As I said, it is a language used by people around the world who need that language to communicate and to express themselves. And the language has changed. The French language used by Aimé Césaire or by Chamoiseau or by Alain Mabanckou in the Congo has nothing to do with the language of Beaumarchais or Voltaire. It's a totally different language, not only because they use different words, but because they make it sing in a different way—you can feel the rhythm, the song. Personally, I feel that in many ways I have been influenced by Creole. I'm not sure—maybe it's my will: I want to be influenced by Creole. I like Creole literature. The way Creole uses simple expressions to mean something more elaborate. For instance, in French, we say "Tel père, tel fils."

GOPNIK: "What a father, what a son."

LE CLÉZIO: Yes, exactly. In Creole, you say, the water runs in the same canal. It means "like father, like son," but it's an image. I like to use this down-to-earth way of speaking. In that sense, I have been influenced by Creole. My grandfather used to talk to me in Creole. There's a long series of questions and answers that you learn as a child in Mauritius, and I still know it by heart.

French literature began a long time ago with, for example, Christine de Pizan, who was Italian, and Rabelais—so many different people.

GOPNIK: Rabelais was a kind of Creole writer, too, wasn't he.

LE CLÉZIO: He was very Creole.

AUDIENCE: Could you tell us something that you learned about writing from another writer, maybe a peer, and also something you learned about writing from a teacher, or somebody older than you?

LE CLÉZIO: I had a very good Greek and Latin teacher. He was sometimes my teacher in French literature as well, and he gave me extraordinary marks. It was the only time in my life I got the best mark for a paper I wrote. So he gave me confidence, because until that time I had no real public. I was writing my short stories, my little novels, giving them to my grandmother, who would say, "Oh this is marvelous." I was not sure about that. This teacher was a great teacher in the old-fashioned way, he was an old-fashioned man. But really a very beautiful mind, a very clear mind and he helped me a lot to get confidence.

AUDIENCE: Your books have a strong social conscience. In your life, are you an activist?

LE CLÉZIO: Not at all, unfortunately. I am a writer, so I live mainly in closed spaces. The period where I was writing outside is over now, I don't do it anymore. I write on an ordinary table in a room in Albuquerque. What I see through my window pane is a place where the tumbleweeds roll, so I don't feel connected, really, to actuality. But sometimes I get indignant, like everyone, about what happens. When bombs were falling on Baghdad, I read in the newspaper that the bombs weighed four thousand pounds. I remembered that the bomb which fell close to my grandmother weighed only one thousand pounds. And I still remember the shake of the explosion. So I can't help thinking, "What do the kids in Baghdad feel when that bomb falls close to them?" I'm not speaking of when it falls on them, but when it falls near them. For their entire life, they will remember it. Those thoughts give way to indignation.

But then, what can I do? I can write novels, and sometimes I put those things in the novels. But I'm often reluctant to sign petitions or to participate in movements, because I have the feeling it would only give self-satisfaction. I would do that and then not think about it anymore. But I still want to think about it, I don't want to forget it. I want to act with my words; it's the only thing I can do. I am not able to go in the streets and yell, I'm not able to wage war against anybody. I don't think I am even able to defend myself against a policeman, so what could I do? But when there were protests against the war in Iraq in Albuquerque, my daughter went and participated and I was very happy that she did. But myself, I must say, I am not a man of action, not at all.

GOPNIK: You raised a daughter of action.

LE CLÉZIO: She is the person of action, she chose that.

AUDIENCE: Have you been influenced by Native American culture?

LE CLÉZIO: Yes, and it began when I was a child. In those dictionaries I mentioned, there were images of Peruvian sculptures and articles on Peruvian civilization, and those made me dream, they made me feel that something extraordinary had happened there and that this extraordinary civilization had completely been wiped out. I wanted to understand how it was possible that it had nearly disappeared. I bought, later, some books about the Inca civilization and the Aztec and Mayan civilizations, and then I had the good luck of doing my military service, in part, in Mexico. The American Indian civilizations, in some ways, had been changed, had disappeared, even, but they are still there. And so, little by little, I read more books, some by Spaniards, some by Indians themselves, by Peruvians. And I felt more and more attracted by these extraor-dinary civilizations—what they had achieved by the time of the conquest by the Spanish, by the French, and by the English.

I mentioned Rita Mestokosho from the Inuit tribe in Québec. She's fighting to protect her valley, the Romaine River Valley, from being wiped out by flooding caused by the Hydro Québec Company. There's a village of about four hundred people fighting against one of the richest, most powerful companies in the world. There is a kind of romanticism in that, but still, I think it's a true and just fight. And most Native Americans have fights which resemble that of Rita Mestokosho: in New Mexico, Arizona, Peru, Ecuador. At the same time, it's interesting to see the interculturality that has been achieved, for instance, in Ecuador, and in Bolivia. The children there are brought up in three languages in school. They have their own native language, another native language, and then Spanish. So intercultural-ity has been achieved in those areas. So if you consider where they have the highest level of interculturality, that would probably be Bolivia and Ecuador.

GOPNIK: And not France or America.

LE CLÉZIO: Not France at all.

GOPNIK: If you can tolerate it, Mr. Le Clézio, I will just read a few brief words of yours. You wrote once—and again I apologize for my translation:

> I am not alone. I know a thousand times over that I am not alone. I only exist physically, intellectually, morally, because of millions of others who exist and have existed around me. This isn't an abstract idea, it's a slice of life, a simple part of reality. And to those others, I owe everything, absolutely everything, my name, my address, my nose, my skin, the color of my hair, my life and my most secret thoughts, my dreams, and even perhaps the place and hour of my death. And in the same manner that I have been formed, I form, and I make. I am at the same time, father, brother, friend, creator, destroyer, murderer. Who knows? To be born is to be plunged into a small universe, where the relations are without number, where each detail, each second that passes is important and leaves its traces.

That seems to me to be as good a model for what literature is, and for what a literary festival can encourage, as any words I know. Thank you for your eloquence.

REBEL SUN

Déwé Gorodé

Translated by Raylene Ramsay and Deborah Walker

Guitar tune at Ulès
when the moon bleaches the waves
evaporating beneath the burning sand
of euphoric nights
Erased images
of our memories betrayed
of our bodies tortured, flayed dispossessed
You are dead indeed
childhood loves
youthful follies
rose-tinted illusions
Already the morning star shines
spiked with a thousand reds
the rays of dawn
blow sky-high
the literary trivia
cock-and-bull bigotry
mindless mouthing
utter rubbish
meaningless babble
the moldy remains of midnight utopias

Behold the return
of the
rebel sun

Camp-Est Prison, October 1974

MEMOIR

THE CALL

Khaled al-Berry

Translated by Humphrey Davies

I descended the mosque steps calmly after the prayer, talking to a friend of mine. The school year had started a few weeks earlier, the university students arriving from their hometowns and the students at the schools returning from their vacations. At the Jam'iya Shar'iya mosque—the Jama'a's main mosque in Asyut—the number of worshipers was huge, larger than any I'd seen throughout the summer vacation. This was my first school year as a committed Muslim with the Jama'a. The atmosphere in the city was tense; the government had decided, as it did on occasion, that Islamist activity had gone too far and had to be stopped. At such times, the mosque would be surrounded by thousands of Central Security troops, who would prevent some preacher or other from giving his sermon or terrorize those who frequented the mosque in the hope that they would decide not to take the risk of going. The huge number of those attending the prayer could act either as a stimulus to the police to interfere or as a deterrent.

On this occasion, it was a stimulus. The buzz of people talking, the sound of their footfalls, the cries of the stall keepers, the attentive expression on my friend's face—all froze, and then suddenly everything exploded. Two agitated hands pushed me from behind, feet stepped on the backs of my shoes, dragging them off my feet. Shots were fired in the air and people knocked into one another like bowling pins, moving together this way and that as though by previous agreement. An acrid smoke got into my nostrils and added to the atmosphere's other ingredients. My face burned, my whole body apparently bursting into flame, just as every atom of the air around me had taken fire all at one go.

I yielded to my instincts and ran away from the shooting, but the roaring of the Central Security soldiers and the deafening sound of thousands of feet pounding the ground to an irregular rhythm started coming from all sides and I didn't know which way to turn. I had the feeling that our house existed in a different world, one separated from me by frightful obstacles. I would run like a madman and enter a building, then retreat and flee again when the residents refused to open their doors and give me refuge. There seemed no escape from the police with their thick, electrified batons. I ran from street to street, forgetting that my age and my face, without beard or mustache, would be enough to hide me from notice so long as I walked normally. One brother from the Jama'a was holding high a crutch belonging to another brother, a cripple who sold perfumes in front of the mosque. He was yelling in the face of the fleeing people, "Stand firm! Your religion is under attack! Defend your Islam!"

I saved the scene in my memory but wasn't strong enough to answer his call. I kept running till I reached our house, where the windows were closed tight to stop the tear gas from the grenades. Through the slanting wooden slats of the shutters I could see the final moments of the battle. The security forces dispersed the people and began chasing those who couldn't run fast enough to get away, beating them viciously while herding them toward the security trucks. My tears weren't because of the gas now. I went to my bed and lay down on my back in the darkened room. I remembered the movies I had watched with the brothers, depicting the first Muslims and their confrontations with the tyranny of the unbelievers. I fell asleep before my tears had dried.

I found myself in a dark, deserted place divided equally into narrow paths that all came together at a circle in the middle. Precisely at the center stood a white dog, which was barking. Dogs had always frightened me, and this dog was barring my return route. I looked all around in the hope of finding a path that would allow me to avoid him. I felt a crippling fear in my legs. I couldn't move. The only light on that dark path was on the other side, but I didn't have the courage to walk past the dog and get to it. Gathering all my strength, I walked on, trembling, impelled only by the certainty that I would perish otherwise. Walking toward the dog, hastening my steps, I said in a loud voice, recalling a song we sang at the mosque, "No, we shall not die cringing for fear of the dogs. No, we shall not die cringing for fear of the dogs."

I woke from my dream still weeping.

FICTION

EL AMANTE DE SEVILLA

Jaime Manrique

In Seville, when I was young, the scent of orange trees in permanent bloom attenuated the sweet reek of bodies buried under rose beds, or at the foot of trees. Sevillanos believed that the loveliest and most fragrant roses and sweetest oranges were those fertilized by the flesh of Nubian slaves. This tang of human decay and fruit trees in bloom was the first thing a visitor noticed upon nearing the city.

The Guadalquivir was barely more than a sandy stream as it ran past Córdoba; but as it got close to Seville, it swelled into a wide olive-colored river. At dawn, the river bustled with barges, swift sloops, feluccas, shallots, tartans, and piraguas. The smaller vessels carried merchandise destined for the bellies of big ships that sailed to the West Indies and beyond. These small boats were like soldier bees that fed the insatiable belly of their queen.

The river fed my wanderlust, making me hunger for the world beyond the confines of the Iberian Peninsula. The river was the road that led to the Mediterranean and the west, to the Atlantic Ocean and the Canary Islands, halfway to the wondrous New World. Young Sevillanos who became sailors, often for the rest of their lives, were referred to as those who had been "swallowed by the sea."

There was no more thrilling sight than the fleets of cargo ships, accompanied by powerful galleons to protect them from English corsairs and privateers, sailing off twice a year for the world Columbus had discovered. If fortune smiled on these adventurers, they would return from the Indies laden with gold and glory.

My eyes bulged as I watched the ox-drawn carts on their way to the royal chambers, carrying open trunks that brimmed with emeralds, pearls, and stacks of blinding bars of silver. Other carts transported bales of tobacco, cocoa, indigo, cochineal, and furs of unknown animals. For weeks after the arrival of the ships, I remained intoxicated. I dreamed of visiting New Spain and Peru.

In the heart of the city, buildings faced each other so closely that I could run down the cobblestone passageways with arms outspread to touch the walls on either side. These were the streets that schooled me in the customs and costumes, religions and superstitions, foods, smells, and sounds of other nations. Merchants arrived in Seville with white, black, and brown slaves from Africa, the Arab countries, the New World. The names of the countries they came from—Mozambique, Dominica, Niger—were as exotic as their looks. I would get dizzy from hearing so many languages that I didn't understand, whose origins I couldn't pinpoint. What stories did they tell? What was I missing? Would I ever get the chance to learn a few of them and visit the places where they were spoken?

During those years, I felt as though I were living in the future, in a city that had nothing to do with the rest of Spain. Pícaros from every corner of the world—false clerics, false scholars, impostors of every imaginable and unimaginable kind, pickpockets, swindlers, counterfeiters, sword swallowers, gamblers, assassins for hire, soldiers of fortune, murderers, whores, fire-eaters, forgers, puppeteers, and snake charmers—came to Seville and made the city their stage. Life there was dangerous and thrilling, as festive and bloody as a bullfight.

Seville was the place where I belonged. It was created for me and I wanted to be its historian. Seville was mine and it owned me.

Most Sevillanos stayed inside during the hottest hours, and went out only at night, when the evening breezes, sweeping up the Guadalquivir from the Mediterranean, cooled the city by a few degrees. Then it was as if a curtain rose, and the proscenium that was Seville became a magical stage for the theater of life. I can still hear in the recesses of my brain the clacking of castanets coming from every street and plaza. The clacking was a reminder to strut with the arrogant elegance of a peacock displaying his colors. People rushed out of their homes to sing on the plazas and dance the salacious zarabandas, which were forbidden by the Church. In the plazas, illuminated by torches, lascivious women, young and old alike, rapped their castanets with fury, turning the instruments into weapons that could seduce and then snuff the life out of you.

The dancers' looks were an invitation to dream about the countless pleasures of the body, and the movements of their hands spoke intricate languages and summoned the spectators with seductive signs. It was thrilling to see the male dancers leap high in the air, spinning in circles, as though to exorcise demons eating them from the inside out. Mid-air, these men seemed half-human, half-bird. From midnight until dawn, the loveliest señoritas were serenaded by their inflamed wooers. Brawls often broke out during these serenatas, and the corpses of unfortunate lovers were found in the mornings, beneath the balconies of their inamoratas, glued to puddles of coagulated blood.

Seville was a city of witches and enchanters. You had to be careful not to cross a woman, because any female—aristocratic or peasant, married or unmarried, old or young, beautiful or ugly, Christian or Moor, slave or free— could have satanic powers. Witches made red roses bloom in their homes in December. They could make or break marriages, could make grooms hang themselves or evaporate on the eve of the wedding, could make pregnant women give birth to litters of puppies.

Unlucky men who crossed the enchantresses were turned into donkeys. As husbands and lovers disappeared, new donkeys materialized and the women who owned these donkeys took delight in making them carry heavy loads. It was common to see a woman whose husband had vanished go around the city addressing every donkey she saw by her husband's name. When an ass brayed in response, the woman would drop on her knees, cross herself, and give thanks to God that she had found her husband. If she wanted her man back, she had to buy the donkey from its owner. Then she would go home, happy to have found her spouse, and spend the rest of her life trying to undo the enchantment. Or she might be just as happy to keep her husband in donkey form. It was said that some of the happiest marriages in Seville were between a woman and her ass.

The Holy Office whipped many women in the public plazas for the extraordinary pleasures they boasted of receiving from their equine lovers. Debauched cries and crescendos of lust traveled to remote villages in the mountains where herds of wild asses brayed with envy. Gypsies took to bringing donkeys that brayed anytime a desperate woman addressed them. If a donkey became erect and tried to mount a young wife who called him by her husband's name, or if a donkey tried to kick a withered harpy who claimed him as her husband, or scurried away when an ugly one threw her arms around his neck, that, too, was considered proof of having found her husband. When a Sevillano allowed inflated notions to swell his head, he was reminded, "Remember, today you are a man, but tomorrow you may well be a donkey."

During Holy Week people did penance for all the sins they indulged in the rest of the year. Then alone would Sevillanos fast and drag themselves on their knees to the cathedral. But Seville's cathedral was not oppressive. It was filled with light, color, ostentatious displays of gold and jewels, illuminated as much by its oil lamps and its candles as by the iridescent light that poured in through its stained-glass windows. It was a place where we went to experience the splendors of the world, not to expiate sins. It seemed to me, as a young man, that God had to be more receptive to our prayers in a place like this, where everybody knew that hope, joy, and beauty were also a part of his covenant with us. I used to walk out of Seville's cathedral content, as if I had just eaten a mariscada and washed it down with wine.

Often, in those days, I escorted my mother on her visits to the cathedral. Our enjoyment of the place was a secret between the two of us that excluded the rest of the family and gave us respite from our dingy house, with its worn-out, second-hand furnishings and leaks in the ceiling of every room. The cathedral's sumptuous altars seemed to relieve Mother, momentarily, of the pain caused by Father's impecuniousness. She loved music above all things. It's true Father played the vihuela at home, but nothing he did gratified her. Only in the cathedral could she listen to music. Her eyes gleamed as the sounds of the clavichord or spinet swelled. Singing made Mother happy. Her voice was clear, and it could hit many of the high notes. I'd only heard it when she sang romances in the kitchen, as she went about her chores, on those occasions when my father left to visit relatives in Córdoba. In the cathedral she would let her voice spill out and rise, with the same abandon and ecstasy I heard in the lament of the flamenco singers.

After church, she would hook my arm in hers, and we would stroll along the banks of the Guadalquivir and stop to gaze at the foreign ships and Armada galleons. One evening, grabbing my hand by the wrist, she implored me, "Don't stay in Spain, Miguel. Go far away from here to some place where you can make a fortune for yourself. In the Indies you will have a brilliant future awaiting you, my son."

She did not mention my father's name, yet I sensed she was pushing me to look for a life completely different from his. Because I was a dreamer, like my father, she feared that, like him, I would become a ne'er-do-well. She had begun to see me as another unrealistic Cervantes male: I would live surrounded by criminals, borrowing reales from my friends and relatives, incapable of putting food on the table. But if I let my imagination flow, the wide waters of the Guadalquivir would eventually lead me to the Indies in the west, or to Italy in the east, or to burning Africa in the south, or to the Orient, beyond Constantinople, to the splendors and mysteries of Arabia, and perhaps even to the fabled court of the Emperor of China.

WHAT GOD GAVE ME
OR, INSTRUCTIONS ON HOW
TO LIVE A NOMADIC LIFE

Cynthia Cruz

Fighter planes carrying American
cigarettes, and sugar in its
diabetic variations: penny candy,
Wonder Bread, and cases of generic
beer. Convoys of trucks bringing fire
water, hundred proof. Antlers, missiles,
clusters of wire, crosses, and rope.
Spurs, skulls, crossbones, and the white
fox of death, stuffed with ripped twenty
dollar bills marked counterfeit. A frayed
rayon tent. War paint, just in case.
Bison leather, horsehair,
a blue tarp, an eagle feather.
A handbook on exile, every page
burned out.

FICTION

RAPTURE CHILDREN

Sigrid Nunez

The first time Cole ever heard of rapture children was at the orphanage, where there were three: a boy and two girls. Rapture children had been around before, but since the pandemic there were lots more of them. Rapture children were children who'd been sent by God to be lights in the coming dark. They would be among the first of the living to be caught up to Jesus' side (right after the holy dead). God had endowed them with special spiritual powers so that they could lead others in the countdown to the Final Battle. Though Pastor Wyatt says there is nothing in the Bible to justify this, his wife Tracy is among those who believe it.

Tracy has a niece named Starlyn who is a rapture child.

The rapture children at the orphanage got so much attention, naturally everyone wanted to be one. Some kids declared themselves raptures and would do almost anything—including lie through their teeth—to prove it. But only grownups could say who was or was not a rapture child.

Cole has heard about rapture children performing heroic deeds and even miracles—the boy at the orphanage was said to have run into a burning house to rescue a baby when he was hardly more than a baby himself—but Cole has never seen anything like that. The older of the two girls said that every night when she knelt to pray Jesus came and stroked her hair. But Cole has learned that seeing Jesus, or at least conversing with him, is not such a rare event.

Some rapture children are unusually gifted. Michaela can read music without having been taught and sings like an angel (there are those who insist rapture children *are* angels). But though everyone says Cole is gifted, too, no one has ever said he might be a rapture child.

One thing all the rapture children Cole has met have in common is that they are good-looking. Almost every one of them is blond. (Michaela's hair is so pale it's more white than yellow; from the back, you might even mistake her for an old woman.)

The biggest difference Cole can tell between rapture children and other children is that raptures have a way of making adults happy without even trying. He has seen Starlyn walk into a room and people light up as they do when dessert is set in front of them. He has heard grown men and women pour out their hearts to twelve-year-old Michaela, asking for her advice about grownup things—should they take this new job, should they have another baby—or for her blessing. The same kind of thing that had happened at Here Be Hope. Some of the other orphans were a little afraid of the rapture children because of this power they had with the adults. And Cole is a little afraid of Michaela. The way she always seems to be either laughing or crying. The way, in church, she is able to keep singing out strong even with tears streaming down her face. A girl with almost no meat on her bones and enormous hungry-looking eyes. There would not have been enough hours in the day for her to fill all the requests she got from people to pray for them.

Cole is afraid of Starlyn, too. But that is love (and a secret).

"Did you used to be one?" Even before he asks Pastor Wyatt this, Cole knows the answer is yes. But Pastor Wyatt gives a loud whoop as if Cole had said something crazy.

"Me? Oh my, no, no, no. I was—my mama would tell you—I was more of a—of a *reptile* child." And when Cole looks confused Pastor Wyatt stops laughing and says, "It don't matter, Cole. It don't matter what kind of child a person is. Like the song goes, Jesus loves all the little children." And he opens the Bible to Mark 10:13, to show Cole where it is written.

At first glance anybody—not just the kids in Bible group—would have found the group leader scary. One of his eyes is dead and lies buried under a patch of purple scar tissue. He has some fierce tattoos—snakeheads, skulls—and his head is shaved like a skinhead's. A silver stud through his right earlobe reminds Cole of a bullet.

Everyone knows Mason Boyle's story because he has told it during the part of Sunday worship when members of the congregation are invited to testify. They know about the fight in the bar where he lost his eye to "this other punk" wielding a broken bottle, and how that was even worse luck than it sounded. As a child Mason had been afflicted with lazy eye, and the vision in that eye had always been blurred and weak. The eye he lost in the fight was his other eye, the one with 20/20 vision.

"I was cast down so low, I hoped to die. I was so mad at the world, if I could've seen 'em I'd have punched out everyone who dared cross my path."

But then Mason started noticing something.

"My left eye—my bad, lazy eye—seemed to be getting stronger."

It took about a year, Mason's hard-working eye making a little more prog-ress each day, until it was as good as his dead eye used to be.

"And then, man, it just kept going! I mean, my left eye actually got *better*. Doctor said she never saw anything like it. Today this here eye is twenty-*ten*!"

Even if they'd already heard the story, people would roar when Mason got to this part. And they would hoot and stomp and clap as he told the rest, so that he had to raise his voice louder and louder.

"It was like God had taken pity on me, and not just a little pity but enough to forgive the fact that I had only myself to blame. Because, don't you know, I *picked* the fight in the bar that night. And I started thinking it was a miracle, and that within that miracle was a message for me. A message about blindness and healing. A message about laziness and strength. A message about work—about doing double duty and being rewarded with brand-new vision.

"And I knew that God was calling on me to put aside all my lazy, shame-ful, devil-delighting habits and to receive what he was holding out: a chance to accept his love and forgiveness and make myself worthy of the vision with which he'd blessed me. Mason the sinner had a new life, and Mason had a mis-sion. Mason was blind no more. Now he must help the blind."

Mason earns his worldly living fixing cars. But, as part of his selfless ser-vice, he helps make Braille Bibles.

Cole likes Mason—all the kids do—and feels foolish for having found him scary. But secretly he wishes he did not have to study Bible with him.

Whenever Pastor Wyatt talks about the Bible, whether he's preaching a sermon or talking on the radio or studying at home alone with Cole, he always makes it sound as if it had all just happened yesterday and he himself had been there. When he tells the story of Jesus, it's as if he'd seen it all with his own eyes—the miracles, the Crucifixion—and Cole is captivated by his big voice and the way he moves his hands, floating them up and down like white birds.

"I'm too deaf to catch most of what he's saying," Cole once heard an old lady in the pew behind him say. "But I feel blessed just watching him."

"You want to teach folks, you got to hold their attention," says Pastor Wyatt. "Won't do if they're bored."

But in Bible group Cole is often bored. In fact, Bible group reminds him a lot of being back in regular school and the kind of assignment he never liked. (*Imagine that you, like the narrator, are drafted into the army to fight a war that you think is wrong. What would you do?*) There is always a topic with a peppy title ("The Beatitudes vs. Bad Attitudes"), and though Mason picks the topic he has a rule about not doing much of the talking. He has another rule, about everyone having to write something about every topic.

"Okay, dudes, listen up. Say a Martian lands on Earth and this Martian comes up to you and he goes, What's this thing you Earthlings call Gospel? How would you define it for him? Say a secular kid tells you his mama told him Jesus' story is nothing but a myth. How would you prove to this kid—without dissing his mama!—that she's wrong? Cite verses but use your own words."

But the worst assignments are the ones that are supposed to be fun. *Rewrite the Beatitudes as hip-hop verses.* The kind of thing that used to make Cole hate school.

But the other kids *do* have fun writing the hip-hop verses. And even when they might not like an assignment, they never get sullen or sarcastic or make a big show of how bored they are. And in this way Bible study is totally different from school. The other kids are happy to be there, and most of them throw themselves into the work. They want to please Mason, and they want to please God. Doesn't Cole?

Mason sees all. Mason is not fooled. Mason teases Cole for not paying attention, for not really trying, and though he does it gently Cole is humiliated, he is ashamed, he knows it's his same old problem. He has always been a bad student. Lazy, like Mason's left eye.

Mason sees all. "Never give up on yourself, little bruh." He texts Cole a message: "Moses was once a basket case."

Cole pictures the Bible that had belonged to his parents, its place on a shelf with other big books: reference books. He remembers his father saying that a person couldn't understand the history of art without some knowledge of the Bible. He remembers his parents and some of their friends playing charades one night after a dinner party, his father having to act out "My God, my God, why hast thou forsaken me?"

He has no idea how much of the Bible either of his parents had read, but he knows that the things that are sacred in Salvation City were never important to them. What Jesus said on the Cross, what happened to the preborn, these were not matters of concern to them.

His parents did not know the truth. They lacked the information. There was no one like Pastor Wyatt to explain the Good News to them. Cole does not understand why it had to be this way. Now that he knows the story of Jesus by heart, he loves Jesus, but he does not believe his parents were treated fairly. Whenever he thinks about it, it's as if some spiny, muscular creature began thrashing around inside him.

Tracy says, "I love this great big beautiful world and I know my life has been blessed. But when I see what's happening out there, all the violence and greed and perversion, well, I understand why it's time for this chapter of the story to end. I want to go where evil can't get its filthy hoof in the door. I want to be with all the people I've ever loved and all the good folks that ever lived, all of us happy together forever with the angels and saints and the Lord."

Everyone in Salvation City talks about being rapture ready. They even *joke* about it. ("Don't cry. It's not like it's not the end of the world.") They talk about the Second Coming and the Resurrection and being reunited with loved ones who've already gone home.

Mason tries to comfort Cole. How did they know his mother and father hadn't seen the light? Who was to say that, at the very last minute, they hadn't taken Jesus into their hearts? How could anyone say for sure that wasn't the way it went down?

Cole could say. For sure, his parents had not done that. And Mason cannot tell a lie. Unless that miracle occurred, Cole's parents would never be with God. And he opens the Bible to John 14:6 to show him where it is written.

Cole would like to talk about it, about why God would have wanted to save him but not his mother and father. He would ask Pastor Wyatt—except it's as if there were an agreement between them not to talk about his parents. Cole has the feeling that, if he himself didn't bring them up now and then, his parents would never be mentioned again. Whenever he starts talking about his life before Salvation City, everybody acts as if the room had suddenly turned too hot or too cold. Now he is learning to be silent. But the spiny, muscular creature goes on thrashing inside him.

MEMOIR

FATHER CHINEDU

Chimamanda Ngozi Adichie

I have always wanted to capture God and put God in a bottle and close the cap tight. I was seventeen when I first said this to a priest. The priest's name was Chinedu and he repeated, "You want to capture God in a bottle?" and began to laugh. He laughed in the most undignified and unpriestly way, his whole body shaking, his head thrown back. Then he stopped and asked, "What kind of bottle? A Coke bottle? Or one of those Lucozade bottles? You think it will be big enough?"

At first I was not sure whether to be amused by his amusement. If I could close that bottle, I told him, then I would no longer have to search for God or doubt God's existence as I had for so long. He looked at me and said that if I ever captured God, then God would no longer be God. "To seek God is to find God," he said.

Father Chinedu was dark-skinned, young, with a muscular build that was close to but not quite stocky. He was the first priest I knew to have an Igbo name. All the others were called Damian or Austin or Francis. He encouraged people to ask him questions during his sermon and sometimes he lost his temper and told them off for being complacent. It was not enough that they came to Mass every Sunday, he said; they also had to care about the people being arrested by the government—this was Nigeria under the Abacha regime.

His irreverence was entirely unselfconscious. In private conversations he called his bishop a joker who was more interested in church collections than in justice. When he was moved to a small parish in the countryside, partly as punishment for speaking out, he changed the standing rule of most Nigerian parishes: You no longer had to pay your dues before you could receive the sacrament.

I was raised a Catholic in a moderate Catholic family. I loved Mass. Kneeling in an incense-scented church at benediction, singing "Tantum ergo

Chimamanda Ngozi Adichie received a 2007 PEN Beyond Margins Award.

sacramentum" often brought me to tears. I loved the drama, the ritual. But for as long as I can remember I have struggled with faith. I have wanted to believe more than I do, longed for the kind of certainty that I saw in people who did not ever think to question the illogicalities of religious teaching. When I first met Father Chinedu—shortly before that conversation about capturing God in a bottle—I was questioning the idea of faith with the intensity of a teenager who had read books about the history of the Catholic Church, and I was close to despair. I did not have the courage or the distance or whatever it took simply to settle for disbelief, and yet I could not convince myself of belief.

Father Chinedu would stop by our house after he'd been to play tennis, and we would sit at the dining table. At first I wanted to scandalize him. I said it was ridiculous that the Pope could wake up one morning and decide that the Blessed Virgin Mary had been taken up into heaven, almost two thousand years after her death, and we were all supposed to meekly agree with this. I said the idea of somebody having to die to save me was silly. Many times Father Chinedu laughed, as if my poking fun at the Church, an institution to which his life was dedicated, was the funniest and most welcome thing. "You know the problem with you?" he asked me once. "You think you have to accept everything. You don't."

I was raised to believe in a God, a white man, whose son, the long-haired image hanging on a wooden cross, had died for me and who had made a place called Purgatory where souls were punished for a while. I changed my idea of God from a blue-eyed white man to a colorless spirit. I found Purgatory childish. Father Chinedu said it did not matter, that I could believe in God and disregard Purgatory, that there were some for whom Purgatory worked and others for whom it didn't, but that was no reason to discount God. "You know what they say about two different routes to the same stream?" he asked. "The stream is still there no matter the path you take." When I pointed out inconsistencies in the New Testament, he didn't try to justify them, he simply said that Saint Paul was an ordinary man and often got caught up in his own ideas of how brilliant he was. I quarreled with the numbingly mechanical rep-etitions of Confession and he said, "If it doesn't do anything for you, then you shouldn't go."

When I told him that I was uncomfortable with the insincerity at the heart of the idea of faith for reward, doing good so as to receive a reward in heaven, he said, "You have to think of those missionaries who were keen to spread their faith. They understood human nature. They knew that they had to make it worthwhile to the people they were trying to convert. But when you do come to know God, you don't need anybody to tell you that it isn't about reward, it's about love." In other words, it was not about striving for heaven, it was about here and now.

I envied Father Chinedu's faith, the resilience of it; his willingness to laugh at the contradictions of it; his confidence in admitting that he did not know; his humility in accepting that he did not need to know; and his ability, despite all this, to say his rosary, recite his psalms, and say, "I look to that man Jesus." Sometimes I asked, "Did that man Jesus even exist?" And he would nod and say, "I think so."

DRAMA

THE MUSEUM OF DREAMS

Nilo Cruz

Cuba, during the Pope's visit. **LUCIANA** is in her thirties, but looks younger, as if a lost childhood has stopped her from aging. **SAMUEL** is the younger brother of **BASILIO**, both in their twenties, and **HORTENSIA** is their mother. **GENERAL VIAMONTE**, in his forties, works for the Interior Ministry.

LUCIANA   I am a traveler about to disembark on the land I left with my brother when I was eleven. But I didn't come here to retrace the past, I came to see the new generation... The new island... (*Sitting on her suitcase.*) I get to a small town called Santiago de las Vegas. I roam around the town... (*Samuel, twenty-four, enters holding a machete and wearing a straw hat.*)

SAMUEL   If you're here to see my mother, you should come in the front gate. It's not polite to wander through private property, without announcing yourself...

LUCIANA   I'm sorry I didn't know...

SAMUEL   Have you come to see my mother?

LUCIANA   No, I was...

SAMUEL   Spying?

LUCIANA   I saw the museum sign.

SAMUEL   Two officers were here yesterday... My mother was right.

Nilo Cruz was awarded the 2009 PEN/Laura Pels Foundation Award for Drama.

Nothing on this island comes in even numbers, so that makes you the third officer...

LUCIANA   I think you're mistaken... I'm not...

SAMUEL   So is the Interior Ministry sending—?

LUCIANA   I'm not from here. I'm a journalist. I'm here for the Pope's visit.

SAMUEL   You are?! (*In a loud voice. Starts calling his brother.*) Basilio... Basilio... Come fast... Come fast... She's here...

LUCIANA   Who are you calling?

SAMUEL   My brother... He'll be very happy to see you. (*Basilio enters. He is a young man in his twenties.*) Come close, Basilio... This lady... She's come to visit us... Call Mamá... The letters worked... She's here with the Pope...

LUCIANA   Wait a minute... I think you're mistaken—

BASILIO   Please, come this way. Our mother will be honored—

LUCIANA   Wait! You're confusing me.

SAMUEL   I'm sorry I confused you... I confused her with the militia, Basilio... Crazy me.

BASILIO   (*Gives him a shove.*) You knucklehead... Bobo... I'm sorry he did that... It's just that the militia has been here a few times because of all the letters we sent abroad. We've had so many problems with the museum, you see.

SAMUEL   One officer was hollering at Mamá... Basilio wanted to cut off his head.

BASILIO   What he's trying to say... We were told that the Pope's tour had been organized and nobody was going to come here.

SAMUEL   We knew they were lying to us because, look, you've come—

BASILIO   They just wanted to close the museum—

SAMUEL   And if Mamá hadn't stood up to that man—

BASILIO   That's enough, Samuel! We still don't know your name...

LUCIANA   ...I'm sorry, I think you're—

BASILIO   But what is your name?

LUCIANA   Luciana Maria.

BASILIO   Luciana... Sounds Spanish.

LUCIANA   I was born here.

BASILIO   You were born here? So that makes you one of us...

SAMUEL   And your last name?

LUCIANA   Harland. (*They react to the foreign last name.*) My husband's
name.

SAMUEL   I'm Samuel and he's Basilio.

BASILIO   We've burdened you with our story...

LUCIANA   No. Not at all... I'm... (*Not finding the words.*) I'm in awe.
(*Both brothers look at each other and laugh at the awkwardness
of the moment.*)

SAMUEL   She's beautiful, isn't she?

BASILIO   Yes. Sorry we confused you.

LUCIANA   Confused is not the word. All of a sudden I don't know
where I am.

BASILIO   You've come here and that's what matters. Welcome to my
mother's house. Welcome to the Museum of Dreams...

(*Sound of a large wave.*)

*

(*Samuel and Basilio have gotten their mother, and now the family stands close to Luciana.*)

SAMUEL   Her name is Luciana Maria… señora Luciana Maria Harland.

LUCIANA   Lucy… You can call me Lucy.

HORTENSIA   Ah, Lucy, better, shorter. I'm Hortensia but they call me Horte. Good for you, too, eh! Hortensia is too long.

SAMUEL   (*Still excited.*) She came from the States, Mamá, just to see us.

HORTENSIA   I knew somebody was coming, the saints told me—

LUCIANA   But you must understand… It was by coincidence I was walking—

HORTENSIA   There's no coincidence, señora Luciana. Nothing is coincidental. Look up the word "coincidence" in the dictionary, "remarkable events," I think it says.

BASILIO   (*Laughs.*) You were sent to us, señora Luciana.

HORTENSIA   I remember telling Basilio about the dream I had the night before. "Something tells me that was a message from the sky… A woman from a foreign country is coming and she will sit here in this room with us…"

BASILIO   It never fails to happen… Mamá's dreams always come true.

HORTENSIA   Samuel was beginning to think that nobody was going to visit us from abroad. I said to him, "Of course somebody is going to come. There is going to be people here from all over the world: cardinals, bishops, reporters… Why wouldn't they be interested in our museum…" We sent letters inviting them to come here.

BASILIO   But we didn't know if they'd be interested in our museum—

HORTENSIA   The museum is not really about dreams... If we were living in another place it would've been called the Museum of Miracles.

SAMUEL   Mamá didn't think the word miracle was right...

HORTENSIA   No. Not for this system we live in, sounded too religious.

SAMUEL   And one night it came to her, right Mamá? A wise spirit whispered the name in her ear... That's how it was, wasn't it?

HORTENSIA   That's right, "The Museum of Dreams," she said... And I thought, That's it. It sounds promising...

BASILIO   Revolutionary...

HORTENSIA   All those things we're always talking about: ideals, dreams, and klin, klan: The Museum of Dreams. (*Laughs at her own inventions.*) Here one has to be inventive, señora Luciana. If you want to survive you have to be clever and figure things out. The Africans say that turtles belong to the fire sign, like scorpions. But turtles are wise, they live in rivers so they don't burn and consume themselves.

BASILIO   There you go again with your African philosophy! What she's trying to say...

HORTENSIA   We are miracle collectors, señora Luciana. We collect what's been omitted and neglected in this country. I've been collecting miracles, before these two were born. It's something that has been passed on to me. There was a woman named Mamá Rita. She was the one who started collecting the miracles. She used to teach the poor to read and write...

SAMUEL   She taught Mamá to read.

HORTENSIA   She used to tell her students that once they had learned to write their blessings, they were literate. That's how the miracles started to be written and collected. The poor used to come from all over with their miracles written on little papers.

SAMUEL   And if they didn't have paper they'd write them on the sleeves of old shirts...

HORTENSIA   Oh, they'd write their blessings on everything, dry leaves, old handkerchiefs... The word got around. But things got ugly with the revolution, all of a sudden it was forbidden to be religious.

BASILIO   But people continued sending their miracles, Luciana...

HORTENSIA   For many years we wanted to build a museum. But it never seemed possible. I used to tell the boys it's not time yet... Not the right time to open a museum...

SAMUEL   Until Mamá said, "Let's open it!"

HORTENSIA   Oh, we got complaints from the locals...

SAMUEL   Complaints? (*Laughs.*) They wanted it closed!

HORTENSIA   They said it was fanaticism! But since the Pope was coming and the whole island was pretending to be religious, I pretended to be a loon and nailed the museum sign outside. (*They all laugh.*) Will you be staying with us, señora Luciana?

LUCIANA   No. I...

HORTENSIA   Please do.

*

(Sound of church bells announcing the morning. Luciana wears a dressing gown. She is listening to music from a Walkman. Hortensia enters with a basin of water and a white towel hanging from her shoulder.)

HORTENSIA   I brought you some fresh mineral water from the springs...

LUCIANA   Oh, señora Hortensia.

HORTENSIA   It's my duty. Fresh mineral water is good for the skin. I see you always carry your music with you.

LUCIANA   Everywhere I go.

HORTENSIA   Oh, I stopped listening to music on the radio. If I turn on the radio, I can't do anything else but sing and dance. And there's always something around here that needs my attention. The saints say that disorder brings confusion and misfortune. I wake up at five, I drink café looking at the last of the moon, then I start my day. (*Luciana has taken off the dressing gown and is now cleaning herself with the water.*) Are you single or married now?

LUCIANA   Divorced.

HORTENSIA   Ah, you're a modern woman.

LUCIANA   Oh no, señora Hortensia, I'm not that modern.

HORTENSIA   Well, you're young and full of life… Here a woman like you not only has to be careful with men, but with spirits. Of course, there are spirits everywhere. In trees, rivers, wandering the streets. There was one spirit who fell in love with me. He must've seen me naked coming out of the bathtub, because I felt his presence like a cold wind. I had to cover myself with a towel. Oh, he followed me for weeks after that. I could feel him behind me like a shadow. He would leave messages everywhere. I'd find rose petals on my sink, or a cat would all of a sudden come into the kitchen with a ribbon in its mouth. And I must say, I liked the attention too. It had been a while since anybody laid eyes on me. All of a sudden, I'd find myself powdering my face in the afternoons. I was putting perfume behind my ears and on my bosom, until I realized what I was doing. And I had to pray to get him away and cleanse my whole being with an egg. Oh, the body never forgets love, Luciana. It has its own time and memories. Sometimes I lie awake at night on that old mattress my husband bought when we got married. I lie there in a hole where the mattress sinks from all those years we made love, and I think to myself, Oh I knew love… I knew love…

And the old days come back, like a forgotten season and restore all of what I was and am.

LUCIANA   Yes, I know…

HORTENSIA   I know you do… I can see it on your face. I can see a man sitting on top of your eyebrows. Am I right?

LUCIANA   You are.

HORTENSIA   And if you don't do something about it, he'll leave footprints all over your features and make wrinkles… The lines from sadness aren't good. The wrinkles from laughter yes, because they till and plow the face… (*Touches her face.*) But it's interesting, you don't have any lines. Let me see the palm of your hand. (*Pause.*) Your hand looks like the hand of a young girl.

LUCIANA   How do you know there's a man?

BASILIO   (*Enters, along with Samuel, holding a tray with coffee cups.*) Breakfast!

SAMUEL   Did you sleep well, señora Luciana?

LUCIANA   Yes, as well as can be. I dreamt that I was walking by a river.

BASILIO   Ah, water… Good. The Ariguanabo River came to greet you.

SAMUEL   Have you met with the Pope many times, señora Luciana?

BASILIO   Samuel, not many people get to talk to the Pope. Maybe they get to kiss his ring.

SAMUEL   But you'll get to meet him now when you go back to the city.

LUCIANA   (*Going along, not wanting to ruin their enthusiasm.*) Well, that's what all the reporters are hoping for…

SAMUEL   Oh, I can just see Luciana sitting in a room with all these men in skirts and all of them whispering about the museum:

One cups his ear, the other one whispers from bishop to bishop and cardinal to cardinal...

HORTENSIA   And after so many holy ears the museum will be blessed! Right, Luciana?

LUCIANA   Well, actually... I've never... It will be my first time... (*All of a sudden she's determined to tell the truth.*) Yes, it will be my first time.

SAMUEL   Even better. The Pope is probably tired of the same priests asking for money to paint their churches...

HORTENSIA   I think we stand a pretty good chance, don't you?

LUCIANA   Of course... Except sometimes I'm not sure what exactly you want me to do...

HORTENSIA   Please come, let us show you... (*The brothers open a panel to reveal a wall full of drawers holding religious objects, such as saints, brass crowns, brass halos, reliquaries, rosaries, ribbons, wooden crutches, silver hearts, silver hands, retablos, etc. It is a magical place that looks like an altar. An angelic aria plays.*) This is the Museum of Dreams...

LUCIANA   My God!

BASILIO   These are just a few of all the miracles that came last month. (*Hands her a file.*)

LUCIANA   May I see... (*Lights change, taking on an ethereal quality. Sound of a Tibetan bell. As Luciana opens the file and begins to read, the person who sent the miracle appears on the stage.*)

FAUSTINO   (*Wears an old straw hat.*) My name is Faustino Angel León. Carpenter and painter residing at Compostela Street, Number 6A... On the ninth of September my father left the country and told me to take his little statue of the Virgin to the wilderness and place it in a river. When I got to the river, and placed the statue in the water, the statue turned into a goldfish, then it turned into a beautiful woman with long hair who disappeared swimming in the green river. She just vanished like sugar in water.

BASILIO   We have subfiles pertaining to the specific miracles the saints have performed. Files on love, work... Then there are cases like this one which we haven't labeled... (*Sound of bell.*)

AMPARO   (*Wears rollers in her hair.*) My name is Amparo de las Rosas. I am a seamstress residing at Cespedes Street. On the seventh of May the only thing my husband and I had to eat was a miserable potato that I fried in a pan with some rancid lard. That night my husband Isidro and I kneeled down in front of the altar and prayed for food. The next morning a flock of birds flew into the house, and I told Isidro to close all the windows to catch some of those God-sent creatures. The house and the patio were full of parrots, turkeys, doves, even birds I'd never seen. That was our miracle because Isidro and I had food for a month. Later that day we heard on the news that an old tree had fallen on a birdcage at the zoo and hundreds of birds had escaped. But those birds that flew into our house weren't from the zoo. That was our miracle.

HORTENSIA   We want the church to acknowledge these miracles, Luciana, and we want you to help us. We want to make the museum a public building.

(*The lights return to normal. Luciana walks to the center of the stage. Basilio closes the panel.*)

BASILIO   (*Approaching Luciana.*) Are you all right?

LUCIANA   Yes... I'd like to talk to you, Hortensia.

HORTENSIA   What is it, Luciana?

LUCIANA   I'm not the right person... It's a mistake... I have to apologize to you.

SAMUEL   You haven't done anything wrong, señora... Did you hear what she said, Mamá?

HORTENSIA   We're the ones who feel awful, Lucy... Our house, the lack of food...

BASILIO   Mamá was saying that if we knew last month that you were coming, we would've killed a pig and roasted it in your honor...

HORTENSIA   We just wish we had more to offer you... We feel bad that you've come from so far... Oh, if we were living in other times, I would've made new curtains and hung them inside the house. We would've painted a little. But nowadays there's no fabric or paint to be found. (*Luciana takes a moment to look at this family.*)

LUCIANA   I don't know what I can do for the museum... But I'll try to do the best I can.

*

LUCIANA   January twelfth. An interrogation with General Viamonte.

VIAMONTE   Señora Luciana Maria, can I see your papers?

LUCIANA   Here's my passport.

VIAMONTE   How long have you been in the country?

LUCIANA   More than twelve days...

VIAMONTE   What's your involvement with the museum?

LUCIANA   I'm simply staying at Hortensia's. Is there a problem, compañero?

VIAMONTE   The new laws don't allow tourists to stay in private homes.

LUCIANA   I'm a journalist, compañero. I'm writing an article about the museum.

VIAMONTE   Is that all you're doing?

LUCIANA   For the moment, yes. Unless there's another place that I should write about.

VIAMONTE   Come with me, compañera.

LUCIANA   Where are you taking me?

VIAMONTE   Come with me.

(*Lights come up on the altar. We hear an Afro-Cuban lullaby.*)

*

LUCIANA   January fifteenth: Midday. A meeting with General Viamonte. (*General Viamonte enters. Luciana covers herself with a shawl. A desk and two chairs are brought on. Luciana and Hortensia sit to the left of the desk. The General walks around as he interrogates Luciana and Hortensia.*)

VIAMONTE   I thought to myself we seem to have an important foreigner in our town.

HORTENSIA   She's not a foreigner, Viamonte... She was born here.

VIAMONTE   She's a foreigner to me! When did you leave, señora?

LUCIANA   1961.

VIAMONTE   Ah! The Pedro Pan flights. The fourteen thousand children that were shipped away to the States... The Pedro Pan project, they called it, like the children's book about the boy who runs away to never-never land and never grows up...

LUCIANA   I thought we were going to talk about the museum!

VIAMONTE   We are. It's very Christian of Hortensia to think that you could do something for this museum... It shows that we haven't managed to abolish the colonial mentality of having foreigners taking care of our problems—

LUCIANA   I think you're mistaken. I took it upon myself—

VIAMONTE   No, I'm not mistaken. When Hortensia came to us with the idea, it appealed to us. Anybody would want to finance a Museum of Dreams. But then—

HORTENSIA   You funded the Museum of Humor that was opened down the road!… I'm sure it took plenty of money to build it.

VIAMONTE   We need to laugh, compañera. We need to laugh at how we live despite all the difficulties imposed on us… It's what keeps us going, our humor.

HORTENSIA   Our faith, compañero… Faith… Go to the river… Go to the seawall in Havana and you'll see how many oblations have been offered to the Virgin of Regla… There's the Procession of Miracles every year.

VIAMONTE   That's once a year, compañera… a few locals celebrating an old tradition…

HORTENSIA   Tradition! It has to do with people who pray who have dreams.

VIAMONTE   But it has nothing to do with tourists coming from afar… It's certainly not about exposing things which tend to be overdrawn, like those silly miracles documented in books.

HORTENSIA   You know well my miracles are simple acts—

VIAMONTE   All miracles have an element of exaggeration! Buddha making five hundred elephants grow out of a lotus flower, Mohammed cutting the moon in two…

LUCIANA   For a man who doesn't believe in miracles, you know more about them than I do.

VIAMONTE   I read about things I dislike, compañera, so I can understand why I feel resistance and aversion. (*Pause.*) We live in an age of reason, of natural science. We take pride in the real. Our system gave me a pair of shoes, a home, a refrigerator. If compañera Hortensia wants to call our accomplishments miracles, then these are the miracles that need to be exhibited in her museum...

LUCIANA   Those are not miracles.

VIAMONTE   Then what are miracles?

LUCIANA   It has to do with faith, compañero.

VIAMONTE   Faith. Faith... And what do you know about faith? You come from a so-called religious land, dollar bills that read: "In God We Trust." What Devil do they worship there? It can't be in the name of God that your country has tried to blockade and starve a small island like ours for years.

LUCIANA   I didn't come here to talk about politics.

VIAMONTE   But you certainly have opinions! How did you get involved in all this religious hysteria? (*Picks up her passport.*) Your visa is strictly for journalistic purposes. Why aren't you in Havana following the Pope?

LUCIANA   Well, I got a letter from Hortensia.

VIAMONTE   (*To Luciana.*) You're lying! The letters she tried to send never left this country. We weren't going to have any commotion around here, compañera. Did you actually think we were going to have the Pope in this town? You live in a world of fantasy, with angels and spirits...

HORTENSIA   No. What happened to my letters! What happened to my letters!

VIAMONTE   You see? Hysteria. That's all this is... Religious hysteria... (*Lights a cigar.*)

HORTENSIA   (*Gathers her strength and rage.*) All these years you've tried to sink me down, to bury me alive. A few days from now all the ceremonies of the Pope will end. Luciana will leave and the two of us will have to live long after all of this is over, in this small town, on this little island. But let me tell you something, compañero, for thirty years I've wanted to spit in your face. Thirty years building up the courage… This froth, and bitter spit in my mouth… But now that I face you, I believe my spit is too clean for your face. If ever I curse anybody in my lifetime then let it be you, Agusto Viamonte. (*Trying to show his indifference, he smokes his cigar.*) May those cigars you smoke burn a hole on your tongue and in your lungs, and may those holes fester. Death I don't wish you. I leave that to God. May you continue to breathe the same simple beautiful air I breathe in this town. Good day, compañero!

*

(*Sound of Luciana's voice reciting articles she has written about the Pope. It's a cacophony of journalistic writing mixed with Gregorian chants. A panel is opened to reveal the museum. Luciana starts looking through the miracles. Sound of bell.*)

HORTENSIA   Reading the miracles?

LUCIANA   Yes. Each one is like a little story. Are you prepared to go to the city today and meet with the bishop?

HORTENSIA   No, I've decided not to go.

LUCIANA   Are you going to let that miserable bastard dictate what to do with the museum?

HORTENSIA   I'm not closing the museum.

LUCIANA   Then do something!

HORTENSIA   The spirits came to me last night and told me that it wasn't the right time…

LUCIANA   And do you believe that is the right thing to do?

HORTENSIA   I'm not giving up, Luciana…

LUCIANA   Then fight. You're strong. I'm sure you can appeal your case.

HORTENSIA   Waiting is a form of fighting.

LUCIANA   (*With contained anger.*) It seems like this whole island is always waiting! Waiting! Waiting for something to happen. And nothing ever happens. Who's going to be the first one to stop waiting! Who's going to be the first!

HORTENSIA   You have your ways… You come from a different world.

LUCIANA   No, I come from the same world.

HORTENSIA   The Pope coming here means nothing. It's all about bringing money to the island.

LUCIANA   You don't know that.

HORTENSIA   I do. I live here. Nothing will change. (*Points to the patio.*) You saw those three white pigeons in the patio this morning when you were hanging your clothes, they were three ladies with large purses who visited my dreams. Messengers who came to me last night.

LUCIANA   (*Losing her patience.*) Oh, Hortensia, I'm sorry, I can't live my life that way! Just give up the museum! Give up on the whole thing! Go ahead and put it in his hands… (*The altar rumbles. A few of the relics fall to the floor.*)

HORTENSIA   That is Elegua, the trickster—the opener of the ways—making noise… He will tell me when to move forward with the museum. Mamá Rita always said, "You must learn to endure what you can't change." (*Luciana realizes that Hortensia and the museum possess higher powers.*)

LUCIANA   You know, Hortensia, I never got any letters from you. One day I just stumbled into this place. Samuel said, "Are you here to see my mother?" And those words must've rung true…

It was by coincidence... (*Catches herself*) No, like you say, there's no coincidence. (*She looks all around her. In silence she's listening to the voices of the miracles.*)

HORTENSIA   Why did you choose to stay with us?

LUCIANA   Because for the moment I needed a sense of place, to belong. And wouldn't you like to live in a place called the Museum of Dreams?

HORTENSIA   I live here. I'm asking you.

LUCIANA   I need to believe that miracles exist. I've been running away from myself...

HORTENSIA   You don't have to tell me... I saw it on your face the first time we spoke.

LUCIANA   I need to believe there is a miracle for me. (*Sound of bell.*)

DIVERSIONS

PISTACHIO, DOWN, AND MY FAT UNCLE

Rivka Galchen

After reading lots of Lydia Davis

PISTACHIO

I'm snacking and I find myself thinking: A pistachio is a bad parable. The ones that are easiest to open are also the tastiest. And the ones that are very difficult to open are generally not fit for eating. Maybe the pistachio is a good parable, for this very reason. Or maybe for another reason. Because it gives the wrong advice, and wrong is right?

This also is not a good parable.

DOWN

I try to think like a shepherd, not like a sheep. That's my way, you see. They try to convince you that times are extremely bad, worse than they are, so that later they can say, look what we did! We fixed it all! That's their M.O. I don't fall for that kind of thing. If I had the money I would be trying to buy my children apartments right now. But I don't have the money. You see: Usually interest rates go down and prices go up, or prices go down but rates go up. Now rates and prices are both down. It's a key time.

Rivka Galchen was a finalist for the 2009 PEN/Robert Bingham Award.

After reading Peter Altenberg

MY FAT UNCLE

For a time, when he was trying to lose weight, he would eat nothing each day except for Twinkies. His oldest brother was a famous heart surgeon, and had performed the first pig heart transplant. His other brother was a physicist who designed the heat shield for the space shuttle. Frank was the youngest and the heaviest. For a while he was selling shoes but he was no good at it. Eventually he went into his family's real estate business, under his brother-in-law's direction, his brother-in-law having been made head of the firm. He had few responsibilities and was looked after financially. I have never heard a story of anyone in the family who didn't like Frank. Frank married and had three kids. He hurt no one's feelings. Then shortly after his sixty-first birthday, he took out an ad in the local newspaper saying that women with large breasts should contact him. A few days later, he flew off in his single-engine plane without sending word of where he was; reports came of him running naked along beaches. He mailed out very expensive gifts to all sorts of people he knew and barely knew. A crystal duck. A pink angora sweater. Within two weeks, his brother, the heat-shield-inventing one, tracked him down. Frank had lost some weight. Bloods were drawn, scans taken, the irregular habits of thyroids considered, the gyri of the brain marveled at in all their ordinariness; the doctors could find nothing wrong with Frank, and sent him home.

Frank apologized, lots. He returned to his life as it was before. Five months later, with no forewarning, he dropped dead in the line of a Piccadilly's cafeteria. It was clear, my mom always said to me, that those two weeks were the best two weeks of Frank's life.

POETRY

ÓYEME, MAMITA

Juan Felipe Herrera

Standing on 20th & Harrison

Tortilla Flats, where railroad tracks still cut across the street, Bekins storage warehouse and the old Regal Select brewery specters over me in reddish smoke rings, this bawdy corner where Tía Alvina ran her Mexicatessen, La Reina, packing tortas de jamón con queso for the truckers while Cousin Chente and me folded coquitos into sharp hot pink and white packs on a steaming iron griddle. Can still hear Cousin Tito in the back of the Victorian slap congas to a Cal Tjader groove at the Black Hawk. Tío Beto upstairs patient and quiet talks to a '50s thick mike in "El Hi-Fi" room, his makeshift studio, recording a Mexican oldies show for Radio KOFY. It's been a while since we've talked, Óyeme. Must be around half past ten. Time for a merienda with pan dulce, right?

Remember when you told me one night in the early '80s, "I am worried about you, Juanito?" And I turned around from my miniature writing table, second floor Capp Street, apartment #10, and froze? Your voice had a ruffled and serious timbre. Recognized it and looked away from the small amber light above my head, "I see you looking at yourself put letters on paper," you said. All my illusions of being a poet shrank, the wings of the eagle-writer that sees all twittered into the shadow of a sparrow, a wavy blot of cold ink on a yellow legal pad.

Juan Felipe Herrera received a 2009 PEN Beyond Margins Award.

REALMS OF POSSIBILITY

PHILIP GOUREVITCH: I've been struck over time that nonfiction writers are often treated the way photographers were treated by the great art museums and art snobs of the early or mid-twentieth century. Just as photography was not accepted as Art—with a capital A—nonfiction is still largely excluded from Literature—with a capital L. Even by writers themselves sometimes: Many novelists who got their start in the '50s and '60s, say, became best known for nonfiction—and they felt resentful if the nonfiction got mentioned first. The big game was to be a novelist. But why cling to such hierarchies? I mean, if you're really trying to respond to the world and to render some account of reality in narrative prose, isn't that what matters? Why is nonfiction still made to sit at the back of the bus?

NORBERT GSTREIN: The difference reminds me a bit of physics before and after the theory of relativity. Classical physics is good enough to express and explain most things. With the theory of relativity, skepticism and ambiguity enter the field—just as in fiction different worlds open up. Fiction is interested in the relativity of the narrator, who is often someone other than the "I." Another distinction might be that a fiction writer has to establish his or her reality, while a nonfiction writer begins with a given reality.

But I find the most interesting type of fiction in the intermediate area, so to speak—fiction filled with facts. W.G. Sebald, Danilo Kiš, Jorge Luis Borges: Those authors mixed fiction and facts and created a new reality. It's not *too* down-to-earth, as some might say against nonfiction, but neither is it a floating reality or a reality without commitment. It is possible, I think, for a fiction writer not to take reality seriously enough. Peter Handke could serve as an example, the way he traveled through the former Yugoslavia and wrote about the Yugoslav Civil War with his head in the clouds. Which suggests that he did not have enough respect for the facts.

COLUM MCCANN: Let's immediately collapse this arbitrary wall between fiction and nonfiction. We might build it up again as the debate goes on. But what does the word "fiction" mean? It comes from *fictus*, to shape. It has noth-

---

This transcript was adapted from "Is Nonfiction Literature?," a public conversation held at the 2009 PEN World Voices Festival of International Literature.

ing to do with reality or nonreality. So why is there a gulf in people's imaginations between nonfiction and fiction—when it's so plain to us that facts are mercenary things? Facts become fiction in so many ways. I will never forget Colin Powell holding up a photograph of a chemical tanker, what, six years ago now, saying, "This is a photograph of a chemical tanker. This is a fact." He extrapolated a fiction from the facts—because he didn't know what was inside that particular tanker, but he told us that chemical weapons were being moved to different parts of the desert. And on the basis of that fiction our daughters and our sons got sent off to war.

I believe that a lot of novelists are now taking stuff from "real life," the facts that are out there and reshaping us, because we doubt what we have been told and how we have been presented with the story—so the job of the novelist right now is to put everything in doubt. And to say, "Question who told you this," "Question why they told you this," "Question why they sent your kids to war," et cetera. We're in the midst of a great age of fictions, I think—an artistic response to how we have been lied to and what we have been told the facts supposedly are.

GSTREIN: In my opinion the big difference between fiction and nonfiction is actually made by the reader. A reader reads nonfiction for information, and fiction for other reasons, which are not quite so easily determined. Nonfiction is about the facts, while with fiction, the question is, really, "Is this a good book or a bad book?"

GOUREVITCH: I disagree with the idea that one reads nonfiction purely for information. Perhaps one reads *bad* nonfiction just for the information—and then quite likely one should distrust the information.

You said earlier, Norbert, that the nonfiction writer has the advantage of a given reality, while the fiction writer has to establish her reality. I'm not convinced of that. I think that the nonfiction writer, too, has to establish a reality—in much the way that Colin Powell did, except that he did it dishonestly, and a writer must do it honestly. I mentioned photography earlier. Photography, too, was dismissed by painters as the mere recording of information. But even with photojournalism—the most deliberately informational mode of photography—one would have to be blind to overlook the individual creator's eye and hand. Consider that photojournalists will often all stand in the same twelve foot space, penned off in front of an event—be it a presidential speech, or Sniper Alley in Sarajevo where they all had to be behind the same six feet of sandbags. And they get very different pictures. From the so-called given reality they establish their individual reality, without any artificial manipulation of the image itself. It is the same with nonfiction. I like to think of the restrictions of nonfiction—the requirement that one sticks to the facts—as a formal challenge. But within the limits, the work can only be done well if one has an imagination as free as any novelist, playwright, or poet.

And, by the way, it would be a mistake to confuse pure factuality with pure truth. *The New Yorker* has a famous fact-checking department, which can be enormously helpful, an ultimate safety net—and yet if you had pieces written only by the methods of fact-checking, and not by a writer with perception and sensibility and judgment, the result would be absurd. I suspect one could write, say, a thousand-word piece that was perfectly fact-checkable and completely untrue.

MCCANN: *The New Yorker* also fact-checks its fiction pretty seriously, and that can drive you nuts, too. It seems to me that the purpose of literature is to come alive in a body, in a time, in a geography, that is not your own. That's the real triumph of literature, whether it's nonfiction, fiction, poetry—any medium: We become alive in that other time and place. I spent a few days in a hospital recently, and I had a chance to reread *Ulysses*. *Ulysses* takes place on June 16, 1904. I was reading about Bloom and Stephen and the citizens in all the pubs together, and it struck me—as it had sort of struck me before, but this time more so than ever—that my great grandfather had walked the streets of Dublin on June 16, 1904. I never met my great grandfather, and I know very little about him, but suddenly he became spectacularly alive in the fiction that had been created by James Joyce. Now my great grandfather was real and can be documented as a "nonfiction fact," so to speak—otherwise I wouldn't be here. But he really meant nothing to me until I read a fiction that had been created around him, in a sense. This interweave, this double helix of fact and fiction, is where the beauty lies. And I don't think nonfiction, as we classically define it, has pushed itself as far as it can go in that direction. It has not pushed itself as far as fiction has.

GSTREIN: I think nonfiction can make big mistakes by not taking fiction seriously. One problematic example is the book *Who Killed Daniel Pearl?* by Bernard-Henri Lévy. There's a scene that describes the decapitation of Mr. Pearl. It's a horrific scene. And the author decides to lay a second track over that scene—he tries to imagine what might have gone on in Mr. Pearl's head during that moment. And, of course, Mr. Lévy has no clue what is going on in this man's head. But he decides that Mr. Pearl is thinking about women during those last moments of his life. The last question Daniel Pearl asks himself, in this version of events, is "What do women really want?"

GOUREVITCH: My understanding is that the book is not presented as fact.

It involves factual investigation and then departs into these fictional reveries. And I suppose to do that right the question is whether one makes those distinctions clear.

GSTREIN: Do you think you can do it?

GOUREVITCH: It's not my thing, but I don't see why it should be taboo. I think the question is whether it can be done successfully and persuasively. There's always going to be the problem that one side or the other is more persuasive. You come away thinking, "Boy, it's better when that guy goes off into fiction," or, "That writer should stick to nonfiction and not put things into his victim's head." James Agee, at the beginning of *Let Us Now Praise Famous Men*—which is one of the really interesting and maddening books that gets assigned to the nonfiction canon—talks endlessly about the value of documentary observation. He's with Walker Evans, embedding, as we now say, with a sharecropper family during the depression for *Fortune* magazine. In his remarkable preamble to the book he writes, "If I could do it, I'd do no writing at all here. It would be photographs; the rest would be fragments of cloth, bits of cotton, lumps of earth, records of speech, pieces of wood and iron, phials of odors, plates of food and of excrement." He writes almost a nonfiction manifesto. Then you turn the page to chapter one, and it begins with this lyrical opening in which everybody's asleep—except, he imagines, the woman of the house, and as he pictures her in his mind's eye, he sees her looking back at him, considering him in some sort of cosmic, erotic reverie. And reading this you think, "Wait a minute! This is pure fantasy. I thought I was getting nothing but the dirt beneath the nails!"

GSTREIN: With fictitious persons one has mostly aesthetic problems. But when real people are concerned, ethical problems present themselves as well.

GOUREVITCH: You mentioned earlier the role that the reader's imagination plays in all of this. I have a young daughter who, whenever she hears a story, asks, "Is that a true-life story?" And she doesn't like one or the other better. She's just trying to understand what is documentary and what is fantasy. I find it interesting because some of the great nonfiction is, of course, memoir, which seems to me to belong to a third category, frankly, between fiction and nonfiction. It's not reported or documented and it involves this complicated thing called memory that's neither fiction nor camera-like documentation. Think of Primo Levi and his memoir of Auschwitz, for example. That's different from a researched book about Auschwitz, or an oral history of Auschwitz. What you get in that book is a voice, a sensibility, in his case, a literary sensibility. The book, halfway through, goes into a meditation on Dante. It's also a memoir in which Levi himself barely exists. At one point in the second volume, he gets sick and comes close to death. He says he's not sure what happened over the next six weeks because he was at death's door. Period. And then he goes back to the stories of people around him.

GSTREIN: I have a daughter as well, a four year old. She accepts it when I say that the sky is blue. And then if I say, "The sky is red" or "The sky is yellow," she is, at first, a little astonished, and then she is impressed that language can do that.

GOUREVITCH: Yes—well, the four year olds aren't our problem. It gets a lot harder with the grown-ups.

MCCANN: I think the most important thing about a memoir or an autobiography is that you get the texture, the spirit of things, absolutely right. Facts by themselves are uninteresting. What's interesting is the human heart. Faulkner, in his Nobel address, said literature is about "the human heart in conflict with itself." If you have on the page your blood, sweat, and tears, and you put down the contradictions that are going on within you, then you'll have written a beautiful book that people will want to read. And they will believe you.

GSTREIN: Because the language tells.

GOUREVITCH: And because people want to believe.

MCCANN: Do you think this country values a story more when it is something that supposedly happened?

GOUREVITCH: That's an interesting question. As a teenager, I basically read only novels—and I read them to learn about the world. There was a generation that learned about sex from novels; I learned a lot about politics. And then, as I got older, I found that contemporary fiction had, to some extent, begun to cede the public sphere to nonfiction. The novel burrowed inward or turned to what was eventually called metafiction—into literary preoccupations and smaller internal spaces. Philip Roth wrote a great essay about this called "Writing American Fiction." He starts by discussing a horrible murder in Chicago, and he addresses the problem of being a novelist who every day picks up a newspaper that's going to have a story wilder than most people's imaginations—a problem that felt new to Roth although Dickens overcame it in his time, as Roth did in his own later work.

MCCANN: One of the contradictions of our times is that when you tell a good story, people say, "It was so good, it could've been fiction."

GOUREVITCH: I think that phrase means a couple of things. One, it means the story is entertaining. And it also makes a distinction between storytelling and lecturing—so you're not simply getting a polemic, you're being introduced to a world that unfolds.

MCCANN: I suppose that people think there should be a sort of rounding-out in fiction—that the story should come to a sort of symphonic end, with a coda, maybe. But the fact of the matter is, in real life, there's no real beginning, there's no end. Our stories don't begin or end anywhere. While in fiction, stories do have a definite beginning and an endpoint—or most fiction does. *Finnegans Wake* doesn't, and other books recently have done that as well. But I think people want a sense of completion that they don't find in real life.

GOUREVITCH: Adrian Nicole Leblanc wrote an extraordinary book of nonfiction called *Random Family* that I cite often. She spent ten years with one family, recording, recording, recording. She would go home at night and leave her tape recorder with the family, and people in this family at three in the morning would get up and start talking into the tape recorder. They would turn it on in the background when they were hanging out. Then Adrian composed a book out of ten years of being inside their lives. And she gets into these realms—of pure whimsy and humor, and of erotic and romantic love—that are usually harder to get at in pure nonfiction. There's that minutiae of life, so much that is hidden. Because generally people just won't tell you about these things. Maybe they won't even tell themselves.

MCCANN: And she's writing about families that were heretofore anonymous. That's another thing about fiction: It goes towards the ones in the dark corner who are not necessarily acknowledged. Good storytelling talks about the small, the unacknowledged.

AUDIENCE: I have a general question about reporting. Do you think when people are talking about themselves to someone—and this is sort of a physics metaphor—does something change because of the act of observation?

GOUREVITCH: I distinguish between what I call professional sources and other people that I write about. With professional sources, it's part of their life to talk to reporters or in some way to be interviewed or written about or seen. They're public figures, if only minor ones. And with them I have a different relationship—which doesn't mean that with such a person, you can't also hit a level where they're speaking outside that capacity, without thinking too much about what's going to come out on paper. Then there are people who have never spoken to the press before—in this country, they're often called "ordinary people." But there's another layer to this: As a foreign reporter, you often write about people in a way that they're unlikely to see. Even the public figures—but especially these so-called ordinary people—are unlikely to encounter your newspaper or magazine or book. It's not going to come back to their country.

When I wrote about Rwanda, this was a country that had very high levels of illiteracy, that had no written language prior to colonialism, but it had a very developed oral tradition. Thanks to that oral tradition, you could meet the most uneducated peasant who would have a structured way of recounting a story. People would say things like, "It was this time of day because we were eating our evening meal and this happened." You could see these almost Homeric mnemonic devices doing their work in a very casual fashion. These were story-tellers who cared about asserting accuracy. And what they wanted, usually, was that the world should know their stories. They'd say, "Please tell the world," as though I had some direct line to the world. The first time I dealt with this I was in the Philippines doing a piece about Vietnamese boat people twenty years after the fall of Saigon. They were stuck in refugee camps in the southern Philippine islands, and word got around that there was an American who'd come. Pretty quickly people thought I was a lawyer and then I was a congressman and then I was a senator. They would say, "When you go back to Washington, will you please tell the people that…" And I was writing for *Granta* magazine, for goodness sake. I didn't know if anybody was going to read my story at all.

In this country, the opposite is true. Ordinary people say, "I got a great angle for you." We live in a very mediatized country. I was covering the election, and when I talked to people at a rally they'd immediately have this kind of media self-regard. There's something very meta here. It doesn't mean you can't get past it, but the idea of, "Look, now I'm finally the guy in front of a reporter," is very much on people's minds.

AUDIENCE: Do you think it's easier for a successful writer of nonfiction to write good fiction or vice versa?

GSTREIN: Two examples come to mind. One would be Susan Sontag, who always struggled to get more acclaim for her novels, which in this country, apparently, were not respected as much—at least until *In America*—as her critical writing and her essays. And then there is Naipaul, who went the opposite way; when he ran into problems with his fiction writing, he began to write travelogues.

GOUREVITCH: Many writers do both, certainly. Fiction writers figure out a way to do a nonfiction project that allows them to go and spend time in a place or do some kind of research or expose themselves to a world that they want to write a novel about. I think for Naipaul, that's a huge part of it. In college, I wrote a play because I passed a poster that said there was a playwriting contest, with three hundred bucks—my rent—as the prize. So I wrote a play and I won the contest—and, as part of the prize, talked to a director about the play. He said something that made a big impression on me. I was about eighteen or nineteen at the time. He said, "You know, I don't understand why there are all these categories nowadays. You've got fiction, nonfiction—poets don't write plays, a playwright is a 'theater person' and not in the English department." And he said, "You know, it used to be"—he had kind of a gravelly old voice— "when I was comin' along, a guy wrote whatever he could make a buck at. You just wrote what you could, and if you had to write for a newspaper for a year, you did. And then you cranked out your novel cycle in verse the next year." It was very liberating for me to think of not having to choose between them, even though they each have their own terms.

GSTREIN: Faulkner, after all the great novels he wrote, said, from the bottom of his heart, he would prefer working with poetry. So there's always that longing for the other.

MCCANN: Though he did write poetry.

AUDIENCE: I work in a bookstore, and after 9/11, people would come in and say, "I can't read fiction anymore, things are too serious, I just want to read nonfiction." Which made me crazy. Then Tariq Ali came to the store and read from *Pirates of the Caribbean*, a book about Latin America. And someone asked him, "If I want to understand the Middle East, what should I read?" And Tariq Ali said, "Read novels. If you want to understand Saudi Arabia, read Abdul Rahman Munif." I also heard David Grossman, who writes fantastic fiction and nonfiction, say that he finds the writing of fiction more meaningful, because when he writes novels, he doesn't know what's going to happen. Everything is changeable and nothing is known in advance. And they create other worlds, so we all don't get stuck in this one reality.

MCCANN: Yes—you step into the realm of possibility. People read novels and want novels because we're not happy with our lives. I don't care how rich, how famous we are: Everybody wants another life. And part of the beauty of creating these new lives is that they weren't there before. Thomas Berger said, "Why do writers write? Because it isn't there."

GSTREIN: Many people don't want just to have another life—they want a second life. And reading endows you with the possibility of this surrogate second life. And the act of reading could also be seen as a revolt against the big scandal—that one has to die.

MCCANN: And you can experience pain in fiction and understand the pain, but it doesn't necessarily have to enter your real life.

GOUREVITCH: You mentioned that people, after 9/11, turned to nonfiction. I know I didn't. I remember people saying, "Nobody's ever confronted such characters before—how can we think about this?" And I went back and reread *Man's Fate*. Malraux imagined a terrorist, who isn't necessarily sympathetic, but he gets you inside that head, and you see it's not a crazy mind. Or go back and read *The Possessed*, by Dostoevsky. My impulse wasn't to read the history of the Taliban. That wasn't going to get me where I wanted to go. And I was going to be reading that anyway because I read the newspaper. I was going to get more about the Taliban than I ever wanted in a short time. There's that famous Adorno line: "to write a poem after Auschwitz is barbaric." To me, that's like saying how can human life and human imagination continue after something this terrible? And the answer is: They must. To get back to Faulkner's Nobel speech, he said, talking about "the end of man," that "when the last ding-dong of doom has clanged... there will still be one more sound: that of his puny inexhaustible voice, still talking."

AUDIENCE: I was thinking, as a psychologist, about what makes for the commonality between good fiction and good nonfiction. And I think that empathy is the key. You referred to "the human heart in conflict with itself." I suppose that's what I mean. You have to empathize with the people you're writing about—and enable the reader to do that, too.

MCCANN: What you say about empathy is so important. If we do not try to imagine the lives of others, we are completely lost. And once, say, the last Holocaust survivor is gone, who tells that story? Well, we create fictions about it. And those fictions will be powerful and valid because that story has to be told over and over and over and over and over again.

NOTES

MIMESIS

David Shields

1

Writing began around 3200 BC.

2

The earliest use of writing was list-making for commercial transactions.

3

In 450 BC Bacchylides wrote, "One author pilfers the best of another and calls it tradition."

4

In the second century BC, Terence said, "There's nothing to say that hasn't been said before."

5

Storytelling can be traced back to Hindu sacred writings, known as the Vedas, around 1400 BC.

6

Homer's *Iliad* and *Odyssey*, circa 800 BC, are epics told in verse, not novels, but nonetheless stories.

7

The aphorism is one of the earliest literary forms—the residue of complex thoughts filtered down to a single metaphor. By the second millennium BC, in Sumer, aphorisms appeared together in anthologies, collections of sayings that were copied for noblemen, priests, and kings. These lists were then catalogued by theme: "Honesty," "Friendship," "Death." When read together, these collections of sayings could now be said to make a general argument on their common themes, or at least shed some light somewhere, or maybe simply all obsess about a topic until a little dent had been made into the huge idea they all pondered. "Love." Via editing and collage, the form germinated into longer, more complex, more sustained, and more sophisticated essayings. The Hebrew wisdom of Ecclesiastes is essentially a collection of aphorisms, as is Confucius's religious musing, Heraclitus's philosophy, Ben Franklin's almanac. These extended aphorisms eventually crossed the border into essay: the diaries of Sei Shōnagon, Anne Bradstreet's letters, Kafka's notebooks, Pound's criticism.

8

The earliest manuscript of the Old Testament dates to 150 BC. Parts of the Bible incorporate "real things" into the text. The laws that have come to make up Mosaic Law, for instance, were undoubtedly real laws before they became canonized. There are bits of song and folk poetry scattered throughout the Old Testament that seem to have had a life independent of scripture. The Samson stories were probably folktales that the Judges storyteller worked into his thesis.

9

It is out of the madness of God, in the Old Testament, that there emerges what we, now, would recognize as the real; his perceived insanity is its very precondition.

10

The New Testament renders, sometimes artistically and often from competing points of view, events that supposedly really happened. Matthew, Mark, Luke, and John all wrote between forty and seventy years after the events in question.

11

In his preface to *The History of the Peloponnesian War*, Thucydides acknowledges that he "found it impossible to remember the exact wording of speeches. Hence I have made each orator speak as, in my opinion, he would have done in the circumstances, but keeping as close as I could to the train of thought that guided his actual speech."

12

Plutarch sometimes bulleted his essays with as many as a hundred numbered sections, eschewing narrative completely and simply listing. His essay "Sayings by Spartan women" itemizes quotations from unknown Spartan mothers, wives, daughters, and widows on a variety of topics without any transitional exposition, interpretation, or any suggestion whatsoever as to how we might read the text or even, for that matter, why.

13

In antiquity, the most common Latin term for the essay was *experior*, meaning "to prove," "to make a trial of," "to know by experience," and to "to know by having tried."

14

The etymology of *fiction* is from *fictio*, which means *fashioning*. Any verbal account is a fashioning of events.

15

Ancient novels were either fantastic—Lucian's *The Golden Ass* tells of a man who turns into a donkey and back into a man—or implausible romantic adventures, such as Chariton's *Chaereas and Callirhoe*.

16

St. Augustine's *Confessions*, written in the fourth century, tells his life through the prism of his newfound faith, reflecting on his sins, begging forgiveness from God. For centuries, the memoir was, by definition, apologia pro vita sua: prayerful entreaty and inventory of sins. During the Renaissance, a hybrid memoir—with a more nuanced relation to the divine—emerged: Montaigne's *Essays*, Pascal's *Pensées*, Rousseau's *Confessions*. Memoir wasn't anymore necessarily what one should know but what one could know. With the posthumous publication in 1908 of Nietzsche's *Ecce Homo: How One Becomes What One Is*, God was gone for good.

17

The Tale of Genji: an eleventh-century Japanese text about court life.

18

In the thirteenth century, French troubadours wrote prose poems about thwarted love.

19

In seventeenth-century France, Madeleine de Scudéry (in *Artamène*) and Madame de Lafayette (in *La Princesse de Clèves*) wrote about the romantic intrigues of aristocrats.

20

Before the Industrial Revolution, culture was mostly local; niches were geographic. The economy was agrarian, which distributed populations as broadly as the land. Distance divided people, giving rise to regional accents, and the lack of rapid transportation limited the mixing of cultures and the propagation of ideas and trends. There was a reason the church was the main cultural unifier in Western Europe: it had the best distribution network and the most mass-produced item—the Bible.

21

The books that form the canon of Western literature (the *Iliad*, the Bible) were understood at the time to be true accounts of actual events. In 1572, when Montaigne set himself the task of naming the "new" brand of writing he was doing in his journals—which later became his books—he came upon the Middle French word *essai*, meaning "trial," "attempt," "experiment." (All of life is an experiment. I love fool's experiments; I'm always making them.) Many of the most important writers in the Renaissance—Montaigne; Francis

Bacon, who imported the essay into English; John Donne, whose sermons mattered much more than his poems—were writers of nonfiction. So secure was the preference for truth that Sir Philip Sidney had to fight, in *Defence of Poesie* (published after his death, in 1595), for the right to "lie" in literature at all.

22

In his retirement, walking the streets of Bordeaux, Montaigne wore a pewter medallion inscribed with "Que sais-je?" ("What do I know?")—thereby forming and backforming a tradition: Lucretius to Rochefoucauld to Cioran.

23

Once upon a time, history concerned itself only with what it considered important: along with the agents of these actions, the contrivers of significant events, and the forces that such happenings enlisted or expressed. Historians had difficulty deciding whether history was the result of the remarkable actions of remarkable men or the significant consequences of powerful forces, of climate, custom, and economic consequence, or of social structures, diet, geography, but whatever was the boss, the boss was big, massive, all-powerful, and hogged the center of the stage; however, as machines began to replicate objects, little people began to multiply faster than wars or famines could reduce their numbers, democracy arrived to flatter the multitude and tell them they ruled, commerce flourished, sales grew, money became the risen god, numbers replaced significant individuals, the trivial assumed the throne, and history looked about for gossip, not for laws, preferring lies about secret lives to the intentions of fate. As these changes took place, especially in the eighteenth century, the novel arrived to amuse mainly ladies of the middle and upper classes and provide them a sense of importance: their manners, their concerns, their daily rounds, their aspirations, their dreams of romance. The novel feasted on the unimportant, mimicking reality. Moll Flanders and Clarissa Harlowe replaced Medea and Antigone. Instead of actual adventures, made-up ones were fashionable; instead of perilous voyages, Crusoe carried us through his days; instead of biographies of ministers and lords, we got bundles of fake letters recounting seductions and betrayals: the extraordinary drama of lied-about ordinary life. Historians soon had at hand all the devices of exploitation. Amusing anecdote, salacious gossip would now fill their pages, too. History was human, personal, full of concrete detail, and had all the suspense of a magazine serial. The techniques of fiction infected history; the materials of history were fed the novelist's greed. Nowhere was this blended better than in autobiography. The novel sprang from the letter, the diary, the report of a journey; it felt itself alive in the form of every record of private life. Subjectivity was soon everybody's subject.

24

The origin of the novel lies in its pretense of actuality.

25

Early novelists felt the need to foreground their work with a false realistic front. Defoe tried to pass off *Journal of a Plague Year* as an actual journal. Fielding presented *Jonathan Wild* as a "real" account. As the novel evolved, it left these techniques behind.

26

The word "novel," when it entered the languages of Europe, had the vaguest of meanings; it meant the form of writing that was formless, that had no rules, that made up its own rules as it went along.

27

In the eighteenth century, Defoe, Richardson, and Fielding overthrew the aristocratic romance by writing fiction about a thief, a bed-hopper, and a hypocrite—novels featuring verisimilitude, the unfolding of individual experience over time, causality, and character development.

28

As recently as 1800, landscapes were commonly thought of as a species of painterly journalism. Real art meant pictures of allegorical or Biblical subjects. A landscape was a mere record or report. As such, it couldn't be judged for its imaginative vision, its capacity to create and embody a world of complex meanings; instead, it was measured on the rack of its "accuracy," its dumb fidelity to the geography on which it was based. Which was ridiculous, as Turner proved, and as nineteenth-century French painting went on to vindicate: Realist painting focused on landscapes and "real" people rather than royalty.

29

The novel has always been a mixed form; that's why it was called "novel" in the first place. A great deal of realistic documentary, some history, some topographical writing, some barely disguised autobiography have always been part of the novel, from Defoe through Flaubert and Dickens. It was Henry James (especially in his correspondence with H.G. Wells) who tried to assert that the novel, as an "art form," must be the work of the imagination alone, and who was responsible for much of the modernist purifying of the novel's mongrel tradition. I see writers like Naipaul and Sebald as making a necessary postmodernist return to the roots of the novel as an essentially Creole form, in which "nonfiction" material is ordered, shaped, and imagined as "fiction." Books like these restore the novelty of the novel, with its ambiguous straddling of verifiable and imaginary facts, and restore the sense of readerly danger that one enjoys in reading *Moll Flanders* or *Clarissa* or *Tom Jones* or *Vanity Fair*—that tightrope walk along the margin between the newspaper report and the poetic vision. Some Graham Greene novel has the disclaimer, "This is a work of fiction. No person in it bears any resemblance to any actual person living or dead, etc., etc. London does not exist."

30

When Thomas De Quincey wrote *Confessions of an English Opium-Eater*, he led his readers to believe that his addiction was behind him; he was taking opium when he wrote the book and continued to take it for the next thirty years. Edmund Gosse's *Father and Son*, written when Gosse was fifty-seven, recounts conversations that purportedly took place when he was eight; people who had known the Gosses protested that Edmund made up these conversations, which of course he had. Orwell's "Such, Such Were the Joys" was denounced for its inaccuracies by people who had been his classmates.

31

In the early nineteenth century, modern industry and the growth of the railroad system led to a wave of urbanization and the rise of Europe's great cities. These new hubs of commerce and transportation mixed people as never before, creating a powerful engine of new culture. The industrial age brought technologies of mass production. Suddenly, the cost of duplication was lower than the cost of appropriation. With the advent of the printing press, it was now cheaper to print thousands of exact copies of a manuscript than to alter one by hand.

Copy-makers could profit more than creators, which led to the establishment of copyright, bestowing upon the creator of a work a temporary monopoly over any copies, encouraging artists and authors to create more works that could be cheaply copied. Authors and publishers, including eventually publishers of music and film, relied on cheap, mass-produced copies protected from counterfeits and pirates by a strong law based on the dominance of copies and on a public educated to respect the sanctity of a copy. This model produced, in the twentieth century, the greatest flowering of human achievement the world had ever seen. Protected physical copies enabled millions of people to earn a living directly from the sale of their art to the audience.

32

In 1830, Emerson was frustrated with sermons, with their "cold, mechanical preparations for a delivery most decorous—fine things, pretty things, wise things—but no arrows, no axes, no nectar, no growling." He wanted to find what he called "a new literature." A German con artist, Johann Maelzel, visited America with a "panharmonicon," an organ without keys. He would crank its heavy silver lever three times, step off to the side, and the machine would spit out an entire orchestra's worth of sound: flutes, drums, trumpets, cymbals, trombones, a triangle, clarinets, violins. After seeing Maelzel's machine perform, Emerson called the new literature he'd been looking for "a panharmonicon. Here everything is admissible—philosophy, ethics, divinity, criticism, poetry, humor, fun, mimicry, anecdote, jokes, ventriloquism—all the breadth and versatility of the most liberal conversation, highest and lowest personal topics: all are permitted, and all may be combined into one speech."

33

In the first half of the nineteenth century, which remains for many a paradise lost of the novel, certain important certainties were in circulation: in particular the confidence in a logic of things that was just and universal. All the technical elements of narrative—the systematic use of the past tense and the third person, the unconditional adoption of chronological development, linear plots, the regular trajectory of the passions, the impulse of each episode toward a conclusion, etc.—tended to impose the image of a stable, coherent, continuous, unequivocal, entirely decipherable universe. To have a name, a character was important, all the more so for being the weapon in a hand-to-hand struggle, the hope of a success, the exercise of a domination. It was something to have a face in a universe in which personality represented both the means and the end of all exploration. The novel of characters, though, belongs entirely to the past; it describes a period: the apogee of the individual. The world's destiny has ceased, for us, to be identified with the rise or fall of certain men, of certain families. The world itself is no longer our private property, hereditary and convertible into cash. Two hundred years later, the whole system is no more than a memory; it's to that memory, to the dead system, that some seek with all their might to keep the novel fettered.

34

"The author has not given his effort here the benefit of knowing whether it is history, autobiography, gazetteer, or fantasy," said the *New York Globe* in 1851 about *Moby-Dick*.

35

In 1859, Darwin's *Origin of Species*, which sold out on the first day it was published, threatened to undo the mathematical legitimacy of the Biblical stories, to explain the unexplainable. The Dewey Decimal system was invented in 1876, although adopted slowly at first. A.E. Houseman said, "The aim of science is the discovery of truth, while the aim of literature is the production of pleasure." Knowledge was exciting, but it threatened to quash imagination and mythology. In 1910, the General Convention of the Presbyterian Church adopted the "Five Fundamentals," a doctrine of five principles underlying Christian faith, a list of dogmas requiring of the faithful adherence to the inerrancy and literal truth of scripture. If we must be governed by the two-dimensional world of fact/fiction, then steps must be taken to ensure that our sacred texts land on the side of fact, that scripture not end up in the fictional cul-de-sac. We must be able to believe.

36

In the second half of the nineteenth century, several technologies emerged: commercial printing technology dramatically improved, the new "wet plate" technique made photography popular, and Edison invented the phonograph. The first great wave of popular culture: newspapers, magazines, novels, printed sheet music, records, children's books. Not only did authors and artists benefit from this model but the audience did, too: for the first time, tens of millions of ordinary people were able to come in regular contact with a great work. In Mozart's day, few people ever heard one of his symphonies more than once;

with the advent of cheap audio recordings, a barber in Java could listen to them all day long. At the end of the nineteenth century, the moving picture gave actors a way to reach a much wider audience, effectively linking people across time and space, synchronizing society. For the first time, not only did your neighbors read the same news you read in the morning, and know the same music and movies, but people across the country did, too. Broadcast media—first radio, then television—homogenized culture even more. TV defined the mainstream. The power of electromagnetic waves is that they spread in all directions, essentially for free.

37

Plot itself ceased to constitute the armature of narrative. The demands of the anecdote were doubtless less constraining for Proust than for Flaubert, for Faulkner than for Proust, for Beckett than for Faulkner. To tell a story became strictly impossible. The books of Proust and Faulkner are crammed with stories, but in the former, they dissolve in order to be recomposed to the advantage of a mental architecture of time, whereas in the latter, the development of themes and their many associations overwhelms all chronology to the point of seeming to bury again in the course of the novel what the narrative has just revealed. Even in Beckett, there's no lack of events, but they're constantly in the process of contesting themselves: the same sentence may contain an observation and its immediate negation. It's now not the anecdote that's lacking—only its character of certainty, its tranquility, its innocence.

38

Collage, the art of reassembling fragments of preexisting images in such a way as to form a new image, was the most important innovation in the art of the twentieth century.

39

After Freud, after Einstein, the novel retreated from narrative, poetry retreated from rhyme, and art retreated from the representational into the abstract.

Author's note: This book contains many unacknowledged quotations; it contains little else. I'm trying to regain a freedom that writers from Montaigne to Burroughs had but that we have lost. The uncertainty about whose words you are reading is not a bug, but a feature. Who owns the words? Who owns the music and the rest of our culture? We do. All of us. Reality cannot be copyrighted.

For sections 1, 5, 15-19, 21 (except for parenthetical statement), 27, and 39 of this essay, see "Almost Famous: The Rise of the 'Nobody' Memoir" by Lorraine Adams, *Washington Monthly*.

For section 4, see *Eunuchus* by Terence.

For sections 7, 12, 22 (first half), and 32, see *The Next American Essay* by John D'Agata; for section 13, see an unpublished manuscript by the same author.

For sections 20 and 23, see "The Art of Self" by Williams Gass, *Harper's*.

For section 26, see *Elizabeth Costello* by J.M. Coetzee.

For section 28, see *For Love & Money* by Jonathan Raban. Raban assures me that Greene's disclaimer in section 29 exists, but I can't find it.

For section 30, see *The Situation and the Story* by Vivian Gornick.

For sections 31 and 36, see "Scan This Book" by Kevin Kelly, *New York Times Magazine*.

For section 33, see *Theory of the Novel* by Michael McKeon.

For section 35, see "The Space Between," an unpublished manuscript by Alice Marshall. The last line of my own book *Black Planet* is "All that space is the space between us."

For section 37, see *For a New Novel* by Alain Robbe-Grillet, which is the book that, in many ways, got me thinking about all of this stuff.

For section 38, see *Dime-Store Alchemy* by Charles Simic.

WELCOME TO TYOSEN™!

Ed Park

Welcome to the world of Tyosen™, a land of awesome magic and hair-raising adventure that you discover *at your own speed*, using the convenience of the postal service! A novel, flexible design lets you strategize *in secret* with fellow players from around the world as you defeat incredible creatures, develop supernatural powers, and uncover fabulous treasure. It's just one of several innovations that make Tyosen™ the most incredible role-playing experience ever developed!

You are not the typical gamer. You've played the rest, and are seeking something that will truly transport you to a fantasy world…where the only limit is your imagination. Tyosen™ is the escape that you've been waiting for!

Created by a dream team led by the one and only Marty Fervor (formerly of TSR; freelance play-tester for Mountains of Moralia, Shibboleth, Vow of the Amber Regent, et al.; two full-length modules published in *Dragon* magazine) and his cousin, James N. Fervor (ex-Chaosium, ex–Roc's Claw Game Labs; veteran dungeon-master at several gaming conventions including the legendary Gen Con), Tyosen™ has already been drawing raves from gaming experts.

White Dwarf magazine's Cara Shinto predicts it will be "among the best gaming systems for the money," and *Adventure Hole*'s lead game critic (anonymous) goes even further: "Groundbreaking."

Every installment of Tyosen™—delivered right to your doorstep or P.O. box—will include a striking new black-and-white image by Berris Honga, whose exquisite artwork has been featured in the pages of *Basilisk* and *Red Kobold!* magazines, on the covers of all of Decimal Games' beloved "Micro-Module" line, and on numerous book covers for DAW=SF, Ballantine SF, Warp9, et al. His expressive originals are highly sought-after by fantasy and fine-art collectors alike. We're honored to showcase his one-of-a-kind depictions of Tyosen™.

But it gets even better: *Every twentieth installment includes a full-color*

Honga posterette, suitable for framing.

And to show our thanks to *you*—one of the first 10 responders to our advertisement—we have a **special offer**. We're slashing our price-per-move fee for the first year, from $5 to *just one dollar!* (Your postage not included.)

That means more moves—more monsters—more adventure. And *less* money down toward your first Honga collectible posterette!

It's an unbeatable value, in *any* universe.

HOW DO I PLAY?

Enough with the exciting praise and tantalizing offers. What *is* this game, exactly? How do you play? What happens when you enter the World of Tyosen™?

First, you will receive a randomly generated set of "vital statistics"—numbers that measure your Brawn (B), Agility (A), Endurance (En), Courage (C), Smarts (S), Education (Ed), and Charm (Ch). Unlike other role-playing games, you'll *also* receive a unique combination of three *Secret Powers* personally selected by the Burrow-chief (either Marty or James N. Fervor). The Secret Powers (SP) can be anything from Ventriloquism to Lycanthropy (i.e., were-wolf transformation) to Invisibility. There are over 200 SPs already created for your Tyosen™ universe, with more in the works. Some are formidable. Others are slight—or so they seem…

Be warned: If used unwisely, SPs can corrupt your perceptions…and turn you into something you didn't anticipate. (Though we should add: *That's part of the fun, too!*)

After studying your stats and your SPs, you then decide what sort of character you'd like to be in Tyosen™. For example, someone with high Courage (C) and Brawn (B), or with the rare SP of *Spidering* (the ability to sprout extra arms during combat) might consider being a warlord or *hwarang* (knight). An above-average Agility (A) score and SPs of, e.g., *Wind-Walking* and *River Moving* would be excellent qualities for a mischievous nature spirit.

There are myriad options: You can play a mystical monk, or devious bandit, or even a double agent who must master the arts of surveillance and disguise.

Indeed, there are as many professions as you can dream of. Bootlegger. Buccaneer. Welder. Beast-trainer. Stable-hand. Forger. Machinist. Archer. Oracle. Musician. Gnome.

No matter which role you decide upon, you are guaranteed a thrilling, mind-expanding adventure that's like nothing you've ever experienced.

As you wander this strange and exotic land of Tyosen™—a place parallel to our own world, and occasionally overlapping with it—you learn more and more about the secrets of its past and the hidden forces that threaten to erupt. Violent battles and supernatural cataclysms are not uncommon—but so are vistas of marvelous beauty and mystery.

Streams of molten silver…A valley filled with hundreds of rainbows…Fish that talk…An old man with his face on backwards (what is he saying?)…The two moons, Immuria and Dak-tösh, which never appear in the sky at the same time, *except on one night every five years…*

Not only is the history and geography revealed to you gradually, but so are the *rules*. They are constantly being added to and altered, and—most importantly—*tailored to your experience*. It's a unique approach to gaming, keeping the environment and challenges supple and keeping you, the player, on his or her toes.

Put another way: It's as though you're reading the best fantasy novel you can imagine—because *you* are the main character. Imagine J.R.R. Tolkien, Parker Edwards, or Fritz Leiber weaving a tale so exclusive that *only you* are privy to its enchanting plot. We sincerely believe that once you try Tyosen™, you won't want to stop.

So what do you say?

Are you ready for adventure?

To receive your character and first turn, send ~~$5~~ *one dollar* in cash to:

TANGUN Games, Inc.
P.O. Box 1902
Emile Bell Station
Portsmouth, NH 03801

See you in Tyosen™!

LARA CROFT

Bożena Keff

Translated by Alissa Valles

from On Mother and the Fatherland

She lies half sunken in the swamps of depression, her open jaws
full of complaint. sometimes lava flows. sometimes the cold ash
sifts—of the Jewish Historical Institute archives,
where once, sorting through the shot and the gassed,
she came across something.
—I found—she intones, looking
straight into nothingness (me, in front of her, on a chair)—a document.
My mother was killed in a forest outside Lvov.
She was shot in the forest. Half a century and I didn't know.

*

She didn't know for half a century, and now she knows!
And she speaks of it in the presence of a random witness.
It happened to be some brunette with crocodile skin gloves,
an agent from a fictional world, Lara Croft, someone like that.
Who's just getting into her sports plane in Hawaii when some old maid
dressed in a ragged cloak gets caught in the propeller. Lara gets out
to help the poor woman, who with her eyes cast in a void informs her
that half a century ago her own mother was shot in the forest.

—But how terrible!
Lara cried out, for she is not without a heart.

FABRICATIONS

Richard Ford & Nam Le

RICHARD FORD: Henry James said that "the terrible *whole* of art is free selection." And that's one of the thrilling things about your work, for me, just seeing where you find a story, which is always where I don't expect you to find it. You trained as a lawyer; I went to law school myself. Do you think legal training encourages habits of mind that writing fiction draws upon or exploits in any way?

NAM LE: I guess there's a certain precision that law encourages—though that precision is not necessarily used for the articulation of anything specific. Quite often the law encourages precise obfuscation—leaving a subject open enough so that no one quite knows what you mean, or pretending you know what you mean when, in fact, you don't, or leaving things in a state of vagueness that doesn't appear vague. And that's been quite interesting to import, at times.

FORD: When you first study the law, you think that you're seeking an answer somehow in the material. When, in fact, there is no answer in the material, but the one that you actually confect, somehow.

LE: I think the way the law works is incredibly honest, because it's up front about the fact that in order to advocate a position, you need to create the rhetorical and evidentiary argument for it. And I think that's important to realize about writing fiction as well. Every piece of prose you write not only has to make the argument for its own existence, it has to persuade the reader to go along with it.

FORD: It has to make a kind of sense.

LE: Yes, but there is no—

This transcript was adapted from a public conversation held at the 2009 PEN World Voices Festival of International Literature.

FORD: —preexisting sense.

LE: Exactly. When you look at common law, for example, it's just full of overturned *ratios*, it's full of overturned *obiters*. And what you realize is that personalities matter. The law is very temperamental in that sense, and a lot of people don't realize that.

FORD: V.S. Pritchett, one of my favorites, said that writers are always trying to define what writers are. He also said that a writer is "a man living on the other side of a frontier." He obviously meant that figuratively, but you've crossed a lot of frontiers—from Vietnam to Australia and Australia on to the rest of the world—and you write about people who have as well. Do you think crossing all these frontiers suits the vocation of a writer? Because one could argue that it didn't—that it might leave you in an eternal nowhere.

LE: I think we're all in an eternal nowhere all the time. And I feel strongly that nowadays, in particular, we all feel ourselves displaced in so many different ways. Whenever a person or a character purports to feel at ease with who and what they are, I tend to lose interest in them. That holds no charge for me. We're always in flux and trying to figure out who and what we are, and why it is that we feel so connected to the things over which we had no control. You know, we had no control over where we were born, which family or ethnicity or socio-economic class we were born into, and yet we feel very strongly, and often unquestioningly, a tribal allegiance to these things. If writers are meant to be on the outside looking in, they're in a better spot now, I think, because all of us have the feeling of being immigrants to ourselves. I can't remember who it was, but some writer said that every day a writer has to create the ground he stands on. The idea of not having a ground, not having a base or bedrock—be it cerebral or physical—is actually quite liberating.

FORD: In your stories there are several moments when people feel a kind of insensitivity to their own interior lives. There's a wonderful moment in the long story set in Australia. There's a bully, and a young character named Jamie looks at him and basically sees nothing there. Something has walled off this young man from his interior life.

LE: I think one of the positive prejudices—though it's still a prejudice—of writers and readers is that there is an equivalent richness to everyone's interior lives, no matter what situation or circumstance or cultural background a person comes from. In fact, one's apprehension and engagement with words corrupts but also enlarges one's interior life. And it's not a popular idea, but there are certain vocations and situations in which you might not have an interior life that's as linguistically adaptable as someone else's. Certainly you won't have the vocabulary or the lexicon that a writer needs to employ in order to bring that interior life to the reader. And so what you're doing as a writer is engaging in a big con, in a sense.

FORD: You fabricate that.

LE: You make it up. And you try to make it authoritative.

FORD: These lummoxes, are they then not susceptible to being characters in your stories?

LE: Absolutely not, no. It's a great attraction, in fact. It's a great challenge. And it's not necessarily an advantage to have an exceptionally linguistic interior life. Because what that highlights is how readily and pervasively language fails us— fails to get any purchase on experience and thought and feeling at all.

FORD: And it's optimistic to take somebody who you would guess, conventionally, doesn't have much of an interior life, and give an interior life to that character.

LE: Sure, but is that an exercise of power? Is that an exercise that's paternalistic or condescending?

FORD: Yes, all of those things.

LE: Right.

FORD: Let me ask you something—and this'll be the only question I ask you about Vietnam. The complexity of your relations with Vietnam are probably best worked out in the body of work that you're beginning to accumulate. Mavis Gallant said to me once, "If we knew what went on between women and men we wouldn't need literature." And if we knew what went on between you and Vietnam, we wouldn't need these stories, perhaps. But are there any narrative forms from Vietnam that you seize upon or that contribute in some way to being a short story writer?

LE: The short answer to that is no. But my conversance with Vietnamese literature and narrative forms is pretty minimal. And I've continually come across silence, stonewalling, and cultural reticence, in talking about all sorts of things.

FORD: In your family?

LE: In my family, in my community.

FORD: Well, that's not endemic to Vietnam.

LE: No. But my mom never told me the story of my birth, for example, until I published this book. It was a strange and somewhat disturbing story involving a monsoon, a rickshaw, and a ritual with a witch doctor—and she hadn't told me this story in the thirty years of my life. Now the stories are beginning to come out. A lot of people in the Vietnamese community are coming up to me and saying, "Mate, do I have a story for you." I've accrued some kind of license from writing a book. And I'm honored to be in that position and I look forward to talking to those people and getting their stories down.

FORD: Sometimes the things that you write turn out to be compensatory for the things that are holes in your experience, or holes in your memory. If you have a hole, you fill it in.

LE: I think there are two impulses: If something is missing then, like you said, you fill it in. But by the same token, if there's a wound or a hurt, then the opposing impulse is to dig into it and to aggravate it, to try to figure out what it is about that wound that gives you the urge to turn it into song.

FORD: I have a friend who's Bengali, a scientist at Oxford and also a novelist. She sent me a paper she wrote not long ago that said, "Science and literature are all about understanding." My hackles go up immediately when I read a sentence like that. When you're talking about that wound that you start picking at, are you trying to understand it? Is literature about "understanding"? Does that make sense to you?

LE: No, that doesn't make sense to me.

FORD: Oh, good. I'm so happy.

LE: You shouldn't take any comfort in that—a lot of things don't make sense to me.

FORD: I take my comfort where I take my comfort.

LE: I'd love to know what you think about this. I read these articles that talk about advances in science—in neuroscience, for example, the science of the brain and consciousness—and it's easy for me as a writer to be quite lazy, to think I operate in a different bailiwick to that, I interrogate consciousness in a different way, a lived way, a deeper way, a way more open to ambiguity. But then I think maybe I'm just in the wrong field. What if people do begin to understand more deeply how memory works, for example? Or how someone's moral calculus works, and how the interaction between that calculus and our upbringing or our conditioning works? And what if they can understand this in a really profound and systematic way? That would render what we do an arbitrary sort of scrabbling around the edges.

FORD: But of all of those ways of apprehending things that are not now apprehensible, all of those things you enumerated that science could do so well—wouldn't they still be operating metaphorically? Wouldn't they still have to posit something where nothing is?

LE: Yeah, yeah. And I think that's one of the beauties of trying to formulate systems of understanding. I think of myself as an unashamed vitalist, a crackpot chemist of words. Biologists and chemists for years and years have posited some élan vital that animates us. No one quite knows what gives life to something. Everything can be in fabulous working order, and yet not work. And physicists constantly posit the existence of all sorts of things.

FORD: Things they can't observe.

LE: Exactly. So that they can make their equations work. Dark matter, dark energy, a cosmological constant. Different dimensions. "This system of understanding is perfect if only we had a sixteenth dimension; then everything would be fine." So if they can get away with it, I reckon so can we.

FORD: It doesn't sound any different from what we ostensibly do. I've got another question. Do politics interest you much as a writer? You've written stories that are at least retinally political. One is set in Tehran in a highly charged revolutionary time. "The Boat," another story, is politically charged. It's not very popular in America to be a political novelist, unless you're a comic novelist. Americans don't generally come to literature for instruction about politics, even in the most spiritual sense. But I wonder if it interests you.

LE: Sure, absolutely. But in a way that's subservient to all the other tough things that make a piece of writing work. Politics never provides an overarching imperative or theme for the writing, but politics deals with how we should best treat one another in the world, and of course that's a meaty and juicy subject. Though sometimes I think we use the word "politics" the way we use the word "emotion." We have a very limited and stupidly shallow idea of what "emotional" means, in our common vocabulary. "Aw, I got really emotional at that point," we say, as though emotion is something that exists on the edge of experience; you're pushed too far and you start tearing up. Sure—but we're awash in an ocean of emotion all the time and we can't escape it. Every single second of our lives is emotional. Instead of having some hierarchical structure between politics and the public and the private, we have to realize that every moment of our lives is political in that sense as well. Not in a programmatic or sloganized sense, but in a very real sense that everything we do is inflected and informed by other people, other systems, other structures—and also what we think, solipsistically, other people will think of what we're doing and thinking.

FORD: Literature in that way is about consequences. It's about the heretofore unknown consequence of how I feel and what that seems to cause, or of what I say or what I do and what that then seems to cause.

LE: Right. Yesterday I was thinking out loud and said that maybe the problem with fiction is human beings, characters. We funnel everything through characters. And when you're dealing with something that involves mass influence and forces that have come about because humans have joined together in unpredictable—or predictable—ways, then it seems like the worst kind of bad faith to think you can allegorize that into a simple human story. But if you diffuse that into many human stories then you diffuse the narrative. Why is it that every single apprehension of some great historical incident or atrocity has to come through the story of this guy or that guy, or this woman who was there, and maybe fell in love with that other person?

FORD: As opposed to how then? Do we not need to apprehend it? The conceit is that we are better able to find our experience in others' experience if we use the formal apparatus of a character.

LE: I don't know. I think maybe we're giving that type of fiction more credit than perhaps it's due.

FORD: Character-based fiction?

LE: Character-based fiction.

FORD: And you write that kind of fiction.

LE: I'm a huge fan of character-based fiction. Don't get me wrong. I think that if you're looking for something which is continuously and inescapably mind-boggling and incalculable, then human consciousness is always going to get you there. But I think there are certain things which happen to people as communities, or as societies, perhaps—and this might not be stuff I'm interested in writing about right now—stuff that really can't be transcribed into the story of one person without becoming forced or overly symbolic—

FORD: Or just dull. I think that's wonderful, to take on the premise that there are such things as characters and say, "Well, maybe there aren't," at least for the purposes of many human experiences. Maybe the whole conceit that there are such things as characters is useless to us. And then you'll come up with something better.

LE: Or maybe you won't. But readers, if they realize that, will at least have that in the back of their minds, and not think that a story between this person and that person is the ambassadorial story for their time and place in history.

FORD: It is a premise that as you get older as a writer, which I have done—

LE: Hey, I'm doing it too!

FORD: No, you're not. You do feel, in fact, that some of the formal features you have gone along with all your life do begin to seem a little threadbare.

LE: What sort of things?

FORD: Well, in essence, what you just said. The implementation of a character in a story begins to feel inadequate to what you might be called to want to write. I think to call that into question is a good thing. It takes a certain kind of intellectual vigor to do that, or innocence, or youth—or desperation.

Okay, this is New York, so you have to feed the lions a little bit. Probably everybody in this room has at least a novel in the drawer, so there are certain kinds of question you just simply have to submit to so that people can nod. What do you wish you did better, as a writer?

LE: I don't mean to be coy, but, I mean, everything.

FORD: But you probably think that there are some things that you do better than others.

LE: And those are the things that I most distrust, actually.

FORD: And therefore, what? Are you going to quit doing them?

LE: No—

FORD: But I don't mean this as a philosophical question. It's a nuts and bolts question, really. For instance, "Oh, I'm not very good at getting characters into and out of rooms."

LE: It's tough.

FORD: It's sort of the heavy furniture lifting of being a writer.

LE: That's one of the things I admire about your fiction, though. There are stretches where you can take thirty pages to get a character into a room—but I'm still reading.

FORD: That's why I'm sitting here asking you these questions, and you're sitting there answering these questions. There's a notion that you're born with certain kinds of talent, for lack of a better term, and that you spend a good deal of your working life trying to beat your head against those things that you weren't naturally equipped to do.

LE: I reckon that, in the ultimate accounting, it's more important for writers to be strong where they're strong, rather than to be strong where they're weak.

FORD: In other words, to do the thing you can do.

LE: Though that's not to say that they should be complacent about the other things. I started out mainly reading and writing poetry, and I'm very susceptible to the lyrical. So when I started writing, that was the most difficult thing to do—to indulge that excess, but also to trammel it and cut it down. And I'm not naturally inclined to structural thinking. So when I was writing these stories, that was where I marshaled all my energy and my troops: thinking about structure. Why put this after that? Why tell it from there instead of from here? Why compress this and increase the pace and tempo there? All that stuff.

FORD: Does that kind of thinking seem extraneous to you? You'd rather not be doing it?

LE: A little bit. And I feel as though that's a dirty little secret. Because the writing that I love, when I read it, everything seems absolutely intrinsic and integral to everything else. So I have an idea of other writers out there who just know. They know a scene should speed up a bit here and stop there and then jump to exposition here. Whereas I'm very conscious of being very conscious of structure all the time. I wish I had a more natural and organic understanding of it.

FORD: I think your stories read that way. Your stories read very organically—I don't see the ribs of your stories very much—

LE: Because there's too much fat on them.

FORD: Well, no, but there's a premise that if I can get you through one sentence to the next sentence, that's as much structure as I need. And you do put one wonderful sentence after another wonderful sentence, which works rather well. I mean, this is a splendid book of stories, a really once-in-a-lifetime book that you come across. It has great, great range, it has delving sympathies and intelligence—and then there are also these wonderful sentences, enviable sentences, in my point of view.

LE: Thank you. One of the catchphrases I write under is, "Think of every sentence as a new opportunity to lose a reader."

FORD: Henry James says, "Tell a dream, lose a reader."

LE: Aw, geez, I've got heaps of dreams in my stories.

FORD: What do you find hardest as a writer? By which I mean sitting down and writing sentences every day. Other than arriving. Arriving is hard.

LE: And starting.

FORD: It's boring.

LE: And the middle. And the end. But the hardest thing is somehow managing this contradiction in me: I have to completely believe in something for it to have any chance of carrying that life or that charge that we're talking about, but I also know there's every likelihood it's not going to be very good at all—or that even if it is good, it's not good within the context of the project you're working on or the sentence you're working on or the character you're trying to characterize. So just having that deep doubt, along with maniacal egotism—thinking I'm a bloody genius to have put this together—that's really hard, I think.

FORD: Umberto Eco, in an interview in *The Paris Review*, said that an intellectual is somebody who, by his writing or by whatever it is he does as an intellectual, contributes to knowledge. Is that what you're doing, when you believe in something, trying to make a contribution to what it is possible to think?

LE: No, no. But I do believe that there is an intelligence that inheres in a sentence and in its syntax and in its parts. And that wisdom can be something you had no conscious idea of before. I do believe that sentences, when they work, stories and narratives, when they work, by definition, they're worthwhile to me. Because, once I've read them, I can't imagine my world of letters being without them. So they're adding to that store of knowledge, certainly. There are other things you read and think, "Yeah, that's great," but the Parnassian landscape I live in can do without them. But I'm not sure about trying to write something in the belief that it's going to add to anything else. When you're writing, sometimes you're the last person to know whether you've done that. And, in fact, I think pretty much everything I've thought and written has probably been thought and written in some form.

FORD: I don't know. I hope not.

LE: I hope not too. The thing about art and writing is you can't get away from it, in a sense. If you were moved, affected, or provoked by something, then it's alive to you, and time doesn't matter—it doesn't matter when it was produced. All that art is simultaneously present in you when you write. It's hubristic to say so, perhaps, but it's inevitable to say that when you're writing, you're engaging in conversation with all those people. And of course it's the people who are good that have stuck in your head. There's no shame in acknowledging that.

FORD: In another *Paris Review* interview, Katherine Anne Porter talks about living in Mexico during the revolution and walking through a courtyard and looking in a window. In the window she saw a pretty woman being paid suit to by a corpulent Mexican revolutionary. And she saw that and went home and wrote a story called "Flowering Judas," a classic American short story. And in the interview she said when she saw that scene, she felt a "commotion" in her—somewhere, her chest, her gut, her brain. Do you undergo anything like that when you encounter an experience that seems possible to write about?

LE: An unfashionable trait I have is, for some reason, I am very good at quarantining life from art. I've traveled a fair bit, for example, and I've seen stuff that would seem relatively conducive to being written about—but my mind doesn't really work that way. I don't think, "Ah, that's grist for the mill." And really, that notion, "Where do you get your ideas from?"—even that formulation rubs me the wrong way, because it reduces fiction to ideas. But what is the idea? If I were to ask you, "What was the idea behind *Independence Day*?" you wouldn't be able to say, or would you?

FORD: I would answer it! Well, I would say that I had an experience which did not have language—because it didn't have a shape, it didn't have an interior, it didn't have a quiddity. And yet from me it called forth the opportunity for language. When I say opportunity, there is something about the way you write sentences—and I know this is the illusion of the sentences rather than the actual fact of writing them—but they seem almost gleeful. Every time I pass from one good sentence of yours to another, I feel this remarkable appetite, whose nature is to say, "Oh good, I'm gonna get to write another one." Or, "Oh good, I'm gonna get to say something else that's going to draw something from me that I haven't had drawn from me before." That's really what I'm getting at. There is this appetite.

LE: Absolutely. And a difficult thing for me is to reconcile myself to this mimetic strangeness, as it were. When I write a sentence, I might detect a certain note or a chord in that sentence. And sometimes I think it's a failing to link that note or chord to something in lived life, so to speak, because it doesn't live in lived life, it exists in that sentence.

FORD: It lives in those words. It's not a report.

LE: Exactly. Even though those words are purporting to point to the world. So I feel like I'm cheating a little bit.

FORD: Why?

LE: Because I get that chord and then, sometimes, the easiest thing to do is to follow that chord and see how it moves.

FORD: Away from where? Toward what?

LE: Well, you don't know. I don't know. But once I've followed that chord, I then pull in the world outside in order to create a housing for that music, in a sense. And that might not actually accord the outside thing a real, deep, meant truth, because I haven't looked at the outside thing and thought, "That's what I'm trying to convey." Instead I'm conveying something that's incredibly lin-guistic *and* inarticulable, and then using the outside world as a tool.

FORD: It's such an important thing for you to say that. I made the mistake of reading Michiko Kakutani's review of your book—more fool me—but one of the things she said was that, in the range of things that you're willing to write about—athletes in Australia, people on a boat coming from Vietnam, a young American woman lost in Tehran—you channel these people, and I thought to myself, "No no no, that is absolutely *not* what you do, you do *not* channel these people. Because that means they exist someplace antecedent and you somehow find a representative language, a place for them on the page." But you've just said that isn't really what it is at all.

LE: No, no, no.

FORD: Good.

LE: No. Not that I have anything against Michiko at all—

FORD: Oh no, nor I!

Apropos of writing sentences, I want to read and then ask you about a sentence from "The Boat," which is a tour-de-force. Here's the passage:

> The first hiding place was behind a house by the river. Uncle told her to climb to the top of a plank bed and stay there, don't go anywhere. She lay with the corrugated aluminum roof just a few thumbs above her head, and in the middle of the day the heat was unbearable. The wooden boards beneath her became darkened and tender with her sweat.

When I read "tender with her sweat," I thought to myself, "I couldn't write that sentence." When you wrote that sentence and the word "tender" arrived toward the end—do you remember how it came about?

LE: Absolutely.

FORD: Oh, good.

LE: When you write, there are times you think, "Yeah, I'm all cylinders firing here." And then other times when you think, "Aw, geez, I'm just filling in the gaps. This is just glue." Most of that passage was a glue bit for me. I really didn't like writing it, and I thought, "I've got to write it because we need to get her from this room to that room."

FORD: The ligatures.

LE: The ligatures, exactly. So what I sometimes do as a trick is try to camouflage the ligature-ish nature of those bits somehow. And one way I might do that is by playing with language.

FORD: You pretty them up?

LE: Sometimes, yeah. Or do something which is slightly bait-and-switch, a bit sleight-of-hand. I have a file where I put things that have occurred to me—snatches of conversation, little phrases. One of those phrases was "tender with sweat." So I'm doing something mechanical and arduous, and thinking, "Okay, I need to go into my storehouse of goodies and hopefully get something that will work."

FORD: You don't know how happy it makes me to hear you say that. Because it bespeaks something that I think people who are interested in being writers, and who are good readers, need to know—that, in some ways, being a writer is kind of a clerical nightmare, right? You're always bumping up against your inadequacies, and then you go looking around for all the stuff you've accumulated to try to find something you can slam in somewhere, to connect the things that you think you know to the next thing that you think you know. As far as I'm concerned, that's where writing exists.

LE: Absolutely. What I described just now was a sort of facetious way of saying that, for some reason, that trope, that word, that procession of syllables carried something for me. And all you're doing is following the charge, really. I needed to create the casing—which was psychological as well as logistical—to carry that moment.

FORD: It's almost like writing rhymed and metered verse, because your mind runs away from the obligation to make something rhyme. It runs away from the obligation to make something metrically sound, towards something that will surprise you. Lowell has a great line. He was working on a poem and the word in the middle of the poem was wrong. This is so typical of writing. So he spent days looking for the right word to plug into his poem and finally couldn't find one. So what he did was he put "not" in front of the verb, and after he had put "not" in front of the verb he left the bad word in place, but it reversed the meaning of the sentence. It also gave the line one extra beat, and therefore he liked it.

LE: Yeah. Sometimes all you're doing is actually following sound and rhythm. The words become almost irrelevant. Well, not irrelevant, but to the side.

FORD: Then you do the finish work: making it make sense.

LE: Yeah.

FORD: Do you review books?

LE: I don't, no.

FORD: Oh, good. Someone after my own heart.

LE: What would you have thought or said if I'd said "Yes"?

FORD: This is about me, not you. I think being the arbiter of your colleagues' work, since most of the time your colleagues' work isn't going to be very good—that's just the nature of the world, it isn't a slam against civilization—and so to make yourself the person who says, "Ha ha! Yes indeed, yes indeed. Oh boy, try again," I just think it's unseemly.

LE: Did you ever write reviews?

FORD: I wrote two back in the early '70s. I felt so demoralized after writing them and I quit writing reviews. I always think giving a colleague a bad review is like driving down the road and seeing a hitchhiker and deciding, rather than pick the hitchhiker up, to run over him.

LE: I get that urge all the time.

FORD: We get that urge. But we don't act on that urge. That's the nature of morality. I'm going to read one more passage from your writing. The first story in your book is called "Love and Honor and Pity and Pride and Compassion and Sacrifice," which is exactly what it's about. It's especially terrific because it's set in Iowa—in the environs of the Iowa Writers' Workshop, and there's perhaps no kiss of death quite so toxic as a writers' workshop story—unless it is a professor's story of falling in love with his student and feeling remorse afterwards. Only, you make this story truly extraordinary. In some ways I thought when I read it, "It's kind of a dare." It's as if you said, "I'm just gonna write this Iowa Workshop story, and I'm gonna make it so good you won't be able to categorize it."

There's a passage where two young-Turk, writers-workshop habitués are talking about the literary landscape they'll be walking off into when they leave dreary Iowa City. Here's what they say:

> We had just come from a party following a reading by the workshop's most recent success, a Chinese woman trying to immigrate to America, who had written a book of short stories about Chinese characters in stages of migration to America. The stories were subtle and good. The gossip was that she'd been offered a substantial six-figure contract for a two-book deal. It was meant to be an unspoken rule that such things were left unspoken. Of course, it was all anyone talked about.
>
> "It's hot," a writing instructor told me at a bar. "Ethnic literature is hot, and important too."
>
> A couple of visiting literary agents took a similar view: "There's a lot of polished writing around," one of them said. "You have to ask yourself, what makes me stand out?" She tag-teamed to her colleague, who answered slowly, as though intoning a mantra, "Your *background* and *life experience*."
>
> Other friends were more forthright: "I'm sick of ethnic lit," one said. "It's full of descriptions of exotic food." Or: "You can't tell if the language is spare because the author intended it that way, or because she didn't have the vocab."

It's unfair to read that passage because it isn't typical of the story. But I kind of had a feeling when I read that passage that you were just throwing the gantlet down a bit. You were just gonna say, "You know, I'm not from where you're from. And I'm just gonna do it better than you can do it."

LE: All I can say is—and I feel this on every level—any time I think about what it is that I'm doing, none of the rules or principles under which I work seem to be consistent. The only one that seems to endure for me is: If it feels hard, if it fills you with dread and reluctance, then that's probably telling you something, that's probably a sign that that's where you should be going. So this story… I mean, I knew I was writing a story about a writer, one who was writing about writing, and who was at an MFA program—*that* MFA program—and complaining about it. A story that invokes the tropes of an abusive father, an alcoholic writer, and a burning drum into which the single copy of a manuscript is thrown at the very end. I mean, there's just one cliché and eye-rolling trope after another. It was horrible—I remember thinking to myself, "What are you doing?" But every time one of those dares, as you say, came up in my head, and seemed germane to where the story needed me to go, I felt as if I had no choice. So, for example, my name is used in that story. Anyone reading just that story would probably think I'm a self-conscious writer in that particular way. But if you read the rest of the book, you'll realize I'm actually allergic to that type of self-consciousness.

FORD: When we spoke earlier you said, "Well, I'm going to say some things that will make me sound very inconsistent."

LE: Right.

FORD: This makes you sound very inconsistent.

LE: I, I'll buy it.

FORD: Good. Because you want to bring as much of yourself as you can to the work.

LE: If pushed to it, I can defend those arguments both ways. And the mere fact that it's difficult for me to think of how people might perceive me, or be offended by this or that, or see it as smug or complacent or whatever—you know, I had to get beyond that.

FORD: That's what the story is for.

LE: Right.

FORD: It's the license that a story permits you—if it's a good story.

CALLING THE CHARACTERS

Nancy Willard

Is this the right house? Shabbier than last time
but when was that? Two weeks ago? Two months?
Have they forgotten me? The door's unlocked,
left open for me or somebody else
who fawns over them, a con man after their money
(do they have any?), who listens to their stories
(have I forgotten them?) over and over again.
How still the house sounds.

They sit on the screened-in porch,
silent as after hearing bad news
or an embarrassing remark. They pay me
no mind. Is it supper already?
When I follow them inside, when I sit
in the one place left for a stranger,
nobody looks at me. Nobody passes me
the plate of cold cuts.

They have not spoken for weeks
but they know I am here.
And now, in voices dipped from a pool
of still water, they say inane things,
talking away at each other, small talk,

though not small, I think, as I listen
to what's left unsaid, as I let myself
into their lives again, as I turn transparent

and they grow stronger, noisier, telling each other
what's on their minds, their words filling me up
till I know what they'll say before they say it.
They talk openly now, glad that I'm listening.
They open their hearts.
I leave my self at the door.
Outside, darkness falls but so what?
By their voices I know them.

I take out my pen and write their story.

FICTION

THE TRADE

Roxana Robinson

On her first visit, Beth thought the waiting room was cold: stiff beige chairs, black and white photographs on the walls. Beth hated it. But she'd been edgy that day, not even certain she was pregnant.

Actually, she was certain. The test had been positive, and she'd done it twice. So in a way she'd known, but she hadn't told anyone, not even Will. It hadn't seemed true in the world until her first appointment here.

The night before, Beth had sat alone in the bathroom, wearing an old t-shirt of Will's. Damon, her four year old, was asleep, Will was on his computer. All day long Beth had been holding the secret in her body, as she picked up Damon from school, stopped for groceries, hefted the heavy bags. She'd wondered about the sudden clench of her stomach muscles—might that dislodge it? It was so tiny, anything might dislodge it. It might disengage on its own, just kick loose and swim away.

Beth imagined the endometrium as a fur throw, dense and soft. The fur-lined she-cup. Where in it was this little mite, this little flicker of an idea, moored, amazingly, in the secret curve of her secret cave, taking root in that luxuriance?

She wasn't completely sure she wanted to be pregnant. She hadn't quite made a decision, though a decision had been made. She had a child who was perfect. Smart, funny, beautiful, already in school. Why change things? How could you give two children the attention you gave one? And she was just starting to teach again; a second child would set her back another five years. They'd talked about it, but they hadn't decided. And there was another reason she hesitated.

She held the testing stick up. In the little window was a bold new line. She stared at it. She was alone with this bold new line, and with that tiny vital mite, burrowing deep. She felt something flooding through her, something so pure and powerful, so rich and elemental, that she couldn't tell whether it was joy or dread.

When she'd had Damon they'd been living in Boston; now in New York she'd needed a doctor. A friend had recommended one, but she wasn't taking new patients. This doctor, Kordel, was her partner.

Dr. Kordel was in her early forties, thin, with short brown hair and colorless light eyes. She wore a white lab coat over her dress.

When Beth came into her office Dr. Kordel looked up over the tops of her rimless glasses. Beth felt a sudden visceral reaction. Wasn't it rude not to look straight at someone? "Look at me directly," Beth thought, furious.

She would have to control herself. These sudden hormonal eruptions—she'd have to restrain them. Beth sat down. The walls were beige but the carpet was deep red, which was somehow disturbing.

"I'm Dr. Kordel." The doctor folded her arms along the edge of the desk. "You're here for a pregnancy exam?"

Beth hadn't said the word yet, though she'd checked it on the form. This was the first she'd heard it spoken.

"Let's get you examined." Dr. Kordel stood up. "Then we'll talk."

The air in the examining room was cool, and Beth shivered, pulling off her sweater. Her breasts were already swollen, and the nipples sensitive, though not in a sexual way. This is what pregnancy did: your pleasure, your inclinations no longer mattered. Your body had its own agenda.

The wrinkled blue gown barely covered her thighs. She tied the strings around her waist—was it already thickening? She sat on the examining table. The cotton gown rubbed against her nipples; any touch now was unpleasant, too much.

She wanted to bury her face in her hands, blocking out the light. What she remembered was her mother's face, in the hospital. Her mother had still been in her same room. It was a shock: you thought of the people in a hospital as alive. Ill, but getting better. Or maybe not getting better, but still alive. Her mother's face had been that strange color, and there was no motion in her.

Beth tried to stop. She did not want to think about it now, before this unknown doctor with her rimless glasses came in to examine her.

It was one of those awful ironies: what she'd wanted most, at her mother's death, was her mother's help. She wanted her mother to comfort her for the loss of her mother. It had been so unfair not to have her mother's presence.

Beth had been told before she went in, but that hadn't lessened the shock. There was the body, in the bed by the window. Beth couldn't help herself.

"Mom?" she said. *Why would she not answer?*

Outside, the sky was overcast but bright, full of glare. Across the East River was a gray line of industrial buildings. The nurse left the room and Beth, hugely pregnant with Damon, was alone with her motionless mother.

Beth had returned to that moment over and over, trying to make it come out right, trying to make her mother turn to her and smile, even weakly, even still laboring under the burden of pneumonia, those awful heaving breaths. Beth wanted to have done something to save her.

What stayed with her, what made a dark weight deep in the center of her, was the fear that she'd made a bargain, without knowing it. That she'd made a choice: her pregnancy, her first child, in exchange for her mother. Was that what had happened?

It was absurd, she knew, but also not absurd. Somewhere there existed a set of scales, precise and absolute, where just this sort of transaction took place. The part of her that knew this could never be seen or mentioned.

There was no one she could ask, no one to whom she could say, "All right, then, I've changed my mind. I won't be pregnant, I'd rather keep my mother."

She knew there had been no choice. She had been pregnant, her mother had died. It had been medical error, bad decisions made during the night. She knew that. She knew that.

Beth took her hands away from her face. Her cheeks were wet; she smoothed them dry.

The door opened and Dr. Kordel came in.

"All set?" Her manner was brusque.

Was that true, was she really brusque, or was Beth impossibly touchy, weepy, pathetic?

Dr. Kordel sat on a wheeled stool.

"Slide all the way down." She stretched on a pair of pale gloves.

Lying beneath Dr. Kordel's swift competent fingers, Beth felt her interior as a separate country. She was helpless. Whatever her body would do it would do. She would be explored and monitored by others, by this cold woman with the rimless glasses. She would give herself over to Dr. Kordel, herself and the tiny mite clinging to the fur pelt. They were in this woman's hands.

Later, in the office, Dr. Kordel looked up as Beth came in. "You're ten weeks pregnant."

"Yes." Beth began to cry. She squeezed her eyes shut and covered them with her hand. Dr. Kordel said nothing. Beth pressed her fingers hard against her eyes, trying to stop. There was kleenex on the desk; she took a tissue and blew her nose.

"Sorry. I'm a bit emotional."

"It's not unusual," Dr. Kordel said, and waited. Her short colorless hair was held on one side with a barrette. "Are you happy about this pregnancy?"

Beth closed her eyes again.

"This is—" She stopped. "It's frightening for me." She waited until her voice was level. "When I was pregnant before, with my son, my mother died."

"I'm sorry," Dr. Kordel said. "That must have been very painful."

Beth nodded. "So being pregnant is frightening."

Dr. Kordel looked down at her hands, then up again. "How did your mother die?"

"Medical error. I went in to the hospital to see her, the last night. She was fine, she was coming home in two days. Something went wrong, she wasn't monitored properly. She died in the middle of the night."

"I'm sorry," Dr. Kordel repeated.

Beth nodded. "Thank you." It was worthless, this exchange.

After a pause, Dr. Kordel said, "You know the two things were not related."

Beth shook her head. "I know they weren't. But I'm afraid they were."

There was another pause.

Dr. Kordel looked down. "What do you want to do? This is your decision."

"Yes, of course."

Outside she called Will. She couldn't wait.

"Hola," he said.

At his voice Beth began to cry again. She turned toward the street, so no one could see. Why had she called, now, like this?

"What's the matter?" Will asked.

"I'm pregnant."

"Yes," Will said, idiotically, and that made her laugh. But she wanted to say, *If I have this baby, will you promise not to die?*

When she was three months along they told Damon. It was Sunday morning, and they were all in bed. Damon was driving a small dump truck over the duvet. They explained: a little brother or sister. The whole time, Damon made a low rumbling engine sound. He watched the truck steadily, though he glanced sideways at his parents, still rumbling.

"Is he listening?" Beth said finally.

Will lay back on his pillow, bare-chested, unshaven, his hair wildly at attention. "He gets it. Boys are different. They don't want to do things head-on."

"Except head-butting."

"Except head-butting." Will closed his eyes.

After a moment Beth said, "Hey."

"I'm not, I'm not. I'm just thinking."

"Well, it's my turn to lie in bed with my eyes shut, thinking. You did it yesterday."

"Okay." Will opened his eyes and grimaced. "Okay. I'm up." He threw back the sheets.

Beth turned over. During these first months, sleep overtook her. She could slide down beneath its depths any time, anywhere. Right now she'd plummet downward for an hour, two, three, as long as Will's good nature held out.

"Come on, buddy," Will said to Damon. "Let's go get some breakfast and let mommy sleep."

As they left, as she moved down into darkness, Beth heard Damon ask, "Can I name it?"

She still didn't like Dr. Kordel. After each visit she complained to Will.

"She's so cold," Beth said. "Why would she become an OB/GYN if she hates women? She's like a man."

Will stood over the skillet, stirring the potatoes. His shirtsleeves were rolled up high on his forearms.

"Excuse me?" he said.

"Not you, not you. You know what I mean. She's like a robot. She never smiles."

"My doctor never smiles at me. He gets all this great news about my annual check-up and he never cracks a grin."

"Oh, shut up. This is different. Why are you being such a jerk?"

"Sorry." Will turned to her. "I don't know what to say. What you're going through is so different from what I'm going through, I have no idea what to say. I want to make you feel better and I end up being an asshole."

Beth sighed. "I have no idea what's really happening. Maybe I'm oversensitive. I have no idea. I feel the way I feel. Anyway, this is different. It isn't an annual checkup."

Will put his arm around her.

"I feel like she's holding me at a distance," Beth said. "She's the woman of science, the rational being. She's gone over to the guys' side, with all the scientists, and I'm stuck with the idiot blondes."

"What would you like her to say?"

"'Beth! You're a miracle! You've carried this genius for another four weeks! Congratulations! *The New York Times* will be calling to interview you!'"

Will put his arm around her again.

"I know it sounds stupid," Beth said. "But when you're pregnant you feel proud. It *is* miraculous."

The thought of seeing Dr. Kordel made Beth sick. She had fallen in love, though.

This was partly what made her so resentful, and partly what made up for it. She'd forgotten about this part of pregnancy, when you've given up your old body, your old life. Your body—hijacked by a daring stranger—is sailing the high seas, and you're on board. You're a captive, and enraptured by the voyage, which takes you further and further into the unknown. Your body takes you over. The stranger inside becomes more and more present. Her new son was amazingly active. Precocious.

One afternoon she took Damon's small hand and put it on her belly. Damon looked up, inquiring. He looked like Will—the long face, the hazel eyes—but new.

"Feel this," she said.

The baby was doing somersaults. Beth looked at Damon, but she was also looking inward, feeling her new son—so insolent, so demanding! She loved it.

Damon watched her face, his resistant hand held on the hard swollen belly. When he felt the movement he jerked away, horror in his eyes.

"No," Beth said gently. She squatted clumsily down. "Feel it. That's what you did, when you were inside me." She smiled. "That's what babies do. He's playing. Put your hand right here." But Damon put his hands behind his back and stepped away.

"Lovey," Beth said, "this is your little brother." She ran both hands over her distended self, but he would not come nearer.

It could not be Damon, she told herself. *The trade could not be Damon.*

At the seven-month checkup, Beth felt smug and proud. She had gained only twelve pounds, and the baby (they called him Burrito, after the Flying Brothers) spent his time rocketing around inside her. Had Damon been so acrobatic? She didn't think so.

After the exam, Dr. Kordel sat before Beth's open folder. Beth waited for praise.

"I'm concerned about your blood pressure," said Dr. Kordel.

Beth frowned. "What about it?"

"It's higher than it should be, and I don't want it to become a problem. I'm going to prescribe a medication."

Beth could feel everything in her body halt.

"Prescribe what?" she asked.

"I'll write it out for you."

Beth was shaking her head. "I'm not sure about this."

Dr. Kordel looked up. "You're not sure about it?" Beth felt her throat narrowing. "I don't want to take any medications. I didn't take anything with Damon. He was fine. We were both fine."

Dr. Kordel folded her hands. "I can't answer for that situation, because I wasn't involved." Her voice was cool. "What I can tell you is that your blood pressure has become elevated. That can result in preeclampsia, which is very serious."

"I know about preeclampsia," Beth said. Did this woman think she was a moron?

On the wall behind Dr. Kordel was a close-up photograph of a mother's face, her baby's belly pressed against her cheek. "It's serious," said Dr. Kordel.

There was a pause. Beth felt her pulse rising. She would stay rational.

"I don't want to take any medication." Her voice was too loud.

"What is it that frightens you about this?"

"I've told you about my mother," Beth said. "I don't want to take any medications."

She could feel fear closing in on her. She was about to start falling through some dark endlessness.

"I know about your mother, Beth," Dr. Kordel said, "but this has nothing to do with her."

"Don't call me 'Beth.' Why should you call me by my first name and I call you by your—Doctor? You can call me Mrs. Webster. Or we can both use our first names. I'm not a child." Her voice was high, she was afraid it would break. She was afraid she'd stumble over the word "infantilizing."

Dr. Kordel's mouth tightened. "I'm happy to use your married name, if you prefer. Whatever happened to your mother—and I'm very sorry about it—had nothing to do with you and me, right now."

"How do you know that? Don't you think her doctor told her he was doing the right thing, too? Don't doctors always think they're doing the right thing? You think your patients are ignorant fools."

Dr. Kordel stood up and folded her arms. "'Ignorant fools' is a very highly charged phrase," she said coldly. "It's absurd to say doctors feel that way about their patients."

She had gone too far, Beth thought, now furious at herself. She'd made her doctor angry, and then what? She was an idiot. But she would not permit the doctor to take over her body. She felt panicky and stupid, like a horse, with someone trying to throw a blanket over her head.

"No, I don't mean that," Beth said, trying to be calm. "But I feel as though I have no choice. That's what I mean."

Dr. Kordel remained standing. "As a doctor, I make recommendations based on my knowledge and training. As a patient, you need to trust me. If you can't do that, you need to make other arrangements."

Beth felt the shock physically. "Other arrangements? What do you mean? Do you mean I should find another doctor? I'm six weeks from delivery. No doctor would take me. What are you saying?"

"I mean that's what you have to think about, if you can't accept my recommendations."

"Are you blackmailing me?" Beth asked, her voice shaking with rage.

"Look," Dr. Kordel said. "I know your mother died because of medical error. I'll tell you something. So did my father." She paused. "He had a stroke and went to the emergency room. The staff knew what was happening, and no one came to see him. No one examined him, no one took him into the ICU for oxygen, and he died, there, in the waiting room."

Dr. Kordel took another breath. "I live with that memory every day. It's one reason I became a doctor." She waited. "I'm concerned about your blood pressure. I want to make sure that it doesn't become a problem. This medication is used routinely during pregnancy." She waited again. "I'm going to prescribe it for you. If you refuse to take it, you must find another doctor. I will not be responsible for this pregnancy if you won't cooperate in making it safe."

Beth folded her hands at the bottom of her belly. She was in free fall, there was nowhere to land. She fought to keep from crying.

"Mrs. Webster, I'm on your side," Dr. Kordel said, her voice quieter. "You must understand this. I'm acting in the interest of your health, and that of your baby. But you must trust me. If you don't, we can't proceed."

Beth nodded. She could not speak. She was trapped. And why did the doctor call her "Mrs. Webster," as though she were a stranger?

"Yes." She kept her eyes on Dr. Kordel's desk, the blotter, the prescription pad, the mug with its university logo. She was afraid if she raised her eyes she'd break down. "All right." After a moment she said, "I'm sorry about your father."

Dr. Kordel frowned. "Thank you."

There was a silence. The door opened and the nurse put her head in. "Dr. Russell's on the phone."

"Please tell him I'll call him back." Dr. Kordel was watching Beth.

Each morning Beth took the pill before she brushed her teeth. Will told her not to worry. Each day she grew huger, and the baby rumpused around inside her. In the sonogram he was now a tiny creature, not a confusing mass. He was growing fast, and she worried that he'd be too big.

But Burrito was healthy, and sometimes she did not worry. Sometimes she found she'd stopped whatever she was doing, standing at the window, in the checkout line, in her bedroom, motionless, in a reverie, a vast ocean of delight. Sometimes she woke in the middle of the night gripped by terror, darkness hooding and blinding her.

At her eight-month checkup Dr. Kordel told her she was fine and the baby was fine. He had stopped growing so fast, though—he'd only gained nine ounces.

"Great," Beth said, "he'll be an easy birth."

"Right."

They were courteous. Not friendly, but not unfriendly. Beth had no other option; she had to trust this doctor. Will was careful, quick to put his arms around her, slow to respond to her touchiness. That made her angry, too.

"I'm not a mental patient, you know," Beth said one morning.

Will shook his head and did not answer. He stood by the front door, briefcase in his hand, ready for the day.

"You act as though I were."

"No, I don't." Will pursed his mouth. He did this when he didn't know what to say. She could see the misery in his face, how much he didn't want a fight right now, just before he left for the office.

"I know you don't." Beth sighed. "I'm really ready for this baby to come."

"Two weeks. Two weeks and he'll be here."

They were not calling him yet by his name, which was Andrew. Out of superstition they still called him Burrito. He was a prodigious kicker, a twister, a turner, an acrobat, though with less and less space in which to perform.

That evening, Will lay on Damon's bed, reading to him. Beth came in and lay down with them.

Will squeezed over, still reading, and she smiled at Damon. She lay on her back, so that when Burrito kicked she could take Damon's hand and put it on her belly. He now allowed her to do this, though he still made a face. She lay with her hands on her high hard belly, waiting for Burrito to start his gymnastics. But he was quiet, and they put Damon to bed without a goodnight twist and squirm.

That night they ordered out. Beth could no longer walk, she waddled. She was ponderous, imprisoned. She was no longer living her own life, in her body, she was merely the servant of this somersaulting baby. He had taken her over.

She woke in the middle of the night. For the last month she'd been sleeping badly, strung taut. Now she lay awake in the semi-dark. In the city, night was never really dark. The clock said ten past four. She turned onto her side.

Sometimes, when she woke in the middle of the night, she thought of her mother. Then she had to fold her hands together, locking them hard, and focus her eyes on something—the Matisse poster, dim in the darkness, or the wedding photograph. She had to hold onto something, had to clench her hands and take long even breaths, so she wouldn't cry. Sometimes fear swept over her in huge waves. The thought of Damon in danger made her close her eyes, her breath turn short. *There was no trade*, she told herself.

Now she put her hands on her belly, spreading her fingers. Burrito was quiet. Maybe it was because she was quiet: babies knew your rhythms. This was time to sleep.

It would happen soon. She was seeing Dr. Kordel every week; a bed was reserved. Things were all right with Dr. Kordel, though she hated the barrette in her limp hair. Dr. Kordel's name was Hilary, according to her medical school diploma. Beth wondered what Hilary did for dinner. Did she cook? Did her husband cook? On her desk were photographs of two grinning children. Was her husband a doctor too? Beth smoothed her belly again. Burrito was quiet.

By six o'clock she was standing in the bathroom, looking in the mirror, her mouth dry with fear. *He was not moving.* Was she certain of this? How often did he move normally? She could not be sure. Maybe he usually didn't move during the night, and she just hadn't noticed it. If she called the doctor it would mean something was wrong. She waited for him to move. She put her hand on the bottom curve of her belly, lifting it a bit. She waited for the movement. Now that it wasn't happening she couldn't remember exactly how it felt. What was it? A lift, inside her? A shift? She waited.

There were huge circles below her eyes. Maybe she was overtired, and the baby was tired, and not moving. *He was not moving.* She leaned over, her hands on the outer rim of the sink.

Will found her there.

"What is it?" he asked.

She looked up. "It's stopped moving."

"For how long?"

"I think all night."

"Jesus. Have you called?"

In his face she could see that she should have.

"I'll call now," she said.

They sat on the bed, waiting for the doctor to call back.

"Come in right now," Dr. Kordel said. "I'll meet you at the hospital."

"I'll take care of Damon," Will said, "call me."

At the hospital, Beth lay on the table in the darkened sonogram room. Jelly was smeared on her stomach. It was cold on her bare skin, and she shivered. A technician, a young dark-haired woman, moved a wand around on Beth's belly, watching the screen. She turned dials and pressed buttons, shifting the view, the focus, sliding the wand over Beth's belly. Beth watched her face.

Dr. Kordel slipped into the room, closing the door behind her. She nodded to Beth, then turned to the monitor. Beth watched her face. Dr. Kordel was frowning. Beth lay counting her breaths, making them long and even. She would not let anything happen just because of her fear. She was counting when

Dr. Kordel spoke.

"Beth," she said, "he's gone."

Beth looked at her, the room growing large.

"There's no heartbeat."

Beth sat up. The room had grown enormous. Everywhere around her was black space. The whole universe was there, she was in falling, there was nowhere to land.

"No," she said.

"I'm sorry, Beth. He's gone."

"No he isn't. You promised."

"I'm very sorry. Something's happened. It looks as though the cord has gotten wrapped around his neck."

There was a long silence.

Now what? Now where in the universe?

Beth looked at the doctor. "I need you to put your arms around me, right now," she said. "You have to put your arms around me now."

Dr. Kordel put her arms around her. Beth closed her eyes. Dr. Kordel's fine hair brushed against Beth's face; the barrette pressed against her temple. Dr. Kordel was small and slight, and in her arms Beth felt huge and swollen. Her bare belly was still smeared with gel.

She could remember the buildings outside the hospital room, the way they had risen up, blocking out the light, the way her mother's face had seemed almost blue. She remembered the way her mother could not hold her.

Dr. Kordel's arms were around Beth's back, her grip gentle, surprisingly strong.

"I'm so sorry," Dr. Kordel said. "This is hard to bear." She was crying, too, Beth could feel her sobs.

There was no trade, Beth understood now, there had never been a trade. There were no scales. The reality was much simpler, much worse: her mother had died, and now her baby had died. Dr. Kordel was right. This was hard to bear. *It was hard to bear.* She felt the high black waves rising around her.

She held on tightly to Dr. Kordel's narrow shoulders and felt herself cradled in the other woman's arms. She should have been in the strong arms of someone who loved her—her husband, or her mother—not this fragile stranger. But she had no choice, there was no choice. There was no trade, there were no scales. You did what you could, you bore up under whatever happened. That was the way it was.

Right now, these were the arms that held her, and Beth burrowed into their shelter, pressing her still-swollen self against this slight body, taking what comfort she could against what was coming.

FROM 'ALAN'S WAR'

Emmanuel Guibert

Translated by Kathryn Pulver

There was something strange about our journey now. It seemed to me that we were far from where we were supposed to be. The officers had orders to press forward, but they had no maps. We kept on going.

There were a lot of accidents, especially at night. Many roads and bridges had been destroyed, and in wartime you don't use your headlights. Some guys died because all of a sudden, in the dark, they'd find themselves at the end of a road and SPLASH, they'd fall in.

Something like that happened to us on a tiny country road, probably somewhere in Bavaria. There was no moon that night. We were driving with blackened lights, meaning we'd covered our headlights with hoods slit down the middle. We couldn't see a thing, but we could be seen by the other vehicles from a distance of perhaps ten feet.

We'd driven for two days and two nights without stopping. Polski was exhausted.

My eyes are closing, I can't drive any more. What do we do?

Marker said to me:

Cope, take his place.

Kulik was afraid of driving the armored car. He drove it very badly.

I wasn't used to driving, especially under those conditions, but I managed.
The road was full of sharp turns.
I was following the jeep ahead of me.

All of a sudden, the jeep was gone.

I said to myself: "Don't think you're imagining things. Stop."

I spoke into the microphone:

I'm stopping because the jeep disappeared.

What do you mean, the jeep disappeared?

The road had crumbled, right where there was a particularly sharp turn.
So instead of making the turn, the jeep had fallen straight down into a giant pit.

It had landed nose down. Its occupants were unharmed, but they were climbing back up the hill terrified we'd be right behind them and run them over.

That's what would have happened if I hadn't had the brains to stop.

Armored cars have winches, so that's how we pulled them back up. The jeep was fine, and we got back on the road.

We drove on all the next day. It was becoming surreal. We kept wondering where we were going. Why were we in such a hurry?

By nightfall, we had arrived at a place where they made us get out of our vehicles, but not to sleep.

We're going on patrol.

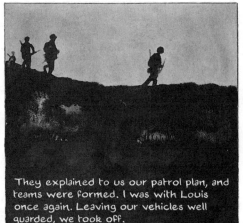

They explained to us our patrol plan, and teams were formed. I was with Louis once again. Leaving our vehicles well guarded, we took off.

Louis was ahead of me. He was carrying the small machine gun, and I had the tripod. Because you had to be flat on your stomach half the time, one person couldn't carry both.

He could have used the machine gun without the tripod in an emergency, although it was pretty heavy. When we had the time, I'd set up the tripod and we'd mount the gun on it.

We formed a long single-file line; there were least 20 of us. We'd gain some ground, then lie flat. We'd gain some more ground, then lie flat again. Our team leader gave us instructions.

Louis was so tired that each time he lay down, he'd fall asleep immediately. I could even hear him snoring.

When it was time to go, I'd hit his feet hard with the tripod to wake him up.

Then I hallucinated – for the first and last time in my life.

On my right there was a long, steep rise of the kind that's typical in areas of rolling hills. I was looking at it.

German bombs, or maybe it was mortar fire, fell in the distance, illuminating the sky at intervals. They didn't reach as far as us, though.

All of a sudden, a gigantic city – huge buildings with brightly lit windows – appeared on the hill.

You had to see it to believe it.

I knew I was seeing something that wasn't there.
I really saw all those lights, as if they were coming
from buildings of different sizes.
It was marvelous.

And then we had to move on again.
I forced myself not to see the city, and it disappeared.

ONE LETTER IS ENOUGH

Liu Xiaobo

Translated by Jeffrey Yang

for Xia

one letter is enough
for me to transcend and face
you to speak

as the wind blows past
the night
uses its own blood
to write a secret verse
that reminds me each
word is the last word

the ice in your body
melts into a myth of fire
in the eyes of the executioner
fury turns to stone

two sets of iron rails
unexpectedly overlap
moths flap toward lamp
light, an eternal sign
that traces your shadow

8. 1. 2000

Liu Xiaobo received the 2009 PEN/Barbara Goldsmith Freedom to Write Award. After co-authoring Charter 08—a manifesto calling for political reform—he was charged with "inciting subversion of state power." If convicted, he faces up to fifteen years in prison.

Jeffrey Yang received the 2009 PEN/Osterweil Award for Poetry.

LONGING TO ESCAPE

Liu Xiaobo

Translated by Jeffrey Yang

for my wife

abandon the imagined martyrs
I long to lie at your feet, besides
being tied to death this is
my one duty
when the heart's mirror-
clear, an enduring happiness

your toes will not break
a cat closes in behind
you, I want to shoo him away
as he turns his head, extends
a sharp claw toward me
deep within his blue eyes
there seems to be a prison
if I blindly step out
of with even the slightest
step I'd turn into a fish

8. 12. 1999

A SMALL RAT IN PRISON

Liu Xiaobo

Translated by Jeffrey Yang

for Little Xia

a small rat passes through the iron bars
paces back and forth on the window ledge
the peeling walls are watching him
the blood-filled mosquitoes are watching him
he even draws the moon from the sky, silver
shadow casts down
beauty, as if in flight

a very gentryman the rat tonight
doesn't eat nor drink nor grind his teeth
as he stares with his sly bright eyes
strolling in the moonlight

5. 26. 1999

DAYBREAK

Liu Xiaobo

Translated by Jeffrey Yang

for Xia

over the tall ashen wall, between
the sound of vegetables being chopped
daybreak's bound, severed,
dissipated by a paralysis of spirit

what is the difference
between the light and the darkness
that seems to surface through my eyes'
apertures, from my seat of rust
I can't tell if it's the glint of chains
in the cell, or the god of nature
behind the wall
daily dissidence
makes the arrogant
sun stunned to no end

daybreak a vast emptiness
you in a far place
with nights of love stored away

6. 30. 1997

DEFINITIONS

THE MEANING OF "SEVERE PHYSICAL PAIN OR SUFFERING"

*The Office of Legal Counsel
of the United States Department of Justice*

The meaning of "severe physical pain" is relatively straightforward; it denotes physical pain that is extreme in intensity and difficult to endure. In our *2004 Legal Standards Opinion*, we concluded that under some circumstances, conduct intended to inflict "severe physical suffering" may constitute torture even if it is not intended to inflict "severe physical pain." *Id.* at 10. That conclusion follows from the plain language of sections 2340-2340A. The inclusion of the words "or suffering" in the phrase "severe physical pain or suffering" suggests that the statutory category of physical torture is not limited to "severe physical pain." *See, e.g., Duncan v. Walker,* 533 U.S. 167, 174 (2001) (explaining presumption against surplusage).

"Severe physical suffering," however, is difficult to define with precision. As we have previously noted the text of the statute and the CAT, and their history, provide little concrete guidance as to what Congress intended by the concept of "severe physical suffering." *See 2004 Legal Standards Opinion* at 11. We interpret the phrase in a statutory context where Congress expressly distinguished "severe physical pain or suffering" from "severe mental pain or suffering." Consequently, we believe it a reasonable inference that "physical suffering" was intended by Congress to mean something distinct from "mental pain or suffering."[1] We presume that where Congress uses different words in a statute, those words are intended to have different meanings. *See, e.g., Barnes v. United States,* 199 F.3d 386, 389 (7th Cir. 1999) ("Different language in

---

[1] Common dictionary definitions of "physical" support reading "physical suffering" to mean something different from mental pain or suffering. *See, e.g., American Heritage Dictionary of the English Language* at 1366 ("Of or relating to the body as distinguished from the mind or spirit"); *Oxford American Dictionary and Language Guide* at 748 ("of or concerning the body *(physical exercise; physical education)").*

separate clauses in a statute indicates Congress intended distinct meanings."). Moreover, given that Congress precisely defined "mental pain or suffering" in sections 2340-2340A, it is unlikely to have intended to undermine that careful definition by including essentially mental distress within the separate category of "physical suffering."[2]

In our *2004 Legal Standards Opinion*, we concluded, based on the understanding that "suffering" denotes a "state" or "condition" that must be "endured" over time, that there is "an extended temporal element, or at least an element of persistence" to the concept of physical suffering in sections 2340-2340A. *Id.* at 12 & n.22. Consistent with this analysis in our *2004 Legal Standards Opinion*, and in light of standard dictionary definitions, we read the word "suffering," when used in reference to physical or bodily sensations, to mean a state or condition of physical distress, misery, affliction, or torment (usually associated with physical pain) that persists for a significant period of time. *See, e.g., Webster's Third New International Dictionary* at 2284 (defining "suffering" as "the state or experience of one who suffers: the endurance of or submission to affliction, pain, loss"; "a pain endured or a distress, loss, or injury incurred"); *Random House Dictionary of the English Language* 572, 1229, 1998 (2d ed. unabridged 1987) (giving "distress," "misery," and "torment" as synonyms of "suffering"). Physical distress or discomfort that is merely transitory and that does not

---

[2] This conclusion is reinforced by the expressions of concern at the time the Senate gave its advice and consent to the CAT about the potential for vagueness in including the concept of mental pain or suffering as a definitional element in any criminal prohibition on torture. *See, e.g., Convention Against Torture: Hearing Before the Senate Comm. On Foreign Relations,* 101st Cong. 8, 10 (1990) (prepared statement of Abraham Sofaer, Legal Adviser, Department of State: "The Convention's wording…is not in all respects as precise as we believe necessary.… [B]ecause [the Convention] requires establishment of criminal penalties under our domestic law, we must pay particular attention to the meaning and interpretation of its provisions, especially concerning the standards by which the Convention will be applied as a matter of U.S. law.… [W]e prepared a codified proposal which…clarifies the definition of mental pain and suffering."), *id.* at 15-16 (prepared statement of Mark Richard: "The basic problem with the Torture Convention—one that permeates all our concerns—is its imprecise definition of torture, especially as that term is applied to actions which result solely in mental anguish. This definitional vagueness makes it very doubtful that the United States can, consistent with Constitutional due process constraints fulfill its obligation under the Convention to adequately engraft the definition of torture into the domestic criminal law of the United States."); *id.* at 17 (prepared statement of Mark Richard: "Accordingly, the Torture Convention's vague definition concerning the mental suffering aspect of torture cannot be resolved by reference to established principles of international law. In an effort to overcome this unacceptable element of vagueness in Article I of the Convention, we have proposed an understanding which defines severe mental pain constituting torture with sufficient specificity to…meet Constitutional due process requirements.").

persist over time does not constitute "physical suffering" within the meaning of the statute. Furthermore, in our *2004 Legal Standards Opinion,* we concluded that "severe physical suffering" for purposes of sections 2340-2340A requires "a condition of some extended duration or persistence as well as intensity" and "is reserved for physical distress that is 'severe' considering its intensity and duration or persistence, rather than merely mild or transitory." *Id.* at 12.

We therefore believe that "severe physical suffering" under the statute means a state or condition of physical distress, misery, affliction, or torment, usually involving physical pain, that is both extreme in intensity and significantly protracted in duration or persistent over time. Accordingly, judging whether a particular state or condition may amount to "severe physical suffering" requires a weighing of both its intensity and its duration. The more painful or intense is the physical distress involved—i.e., the closer it approaches the level of severe physical pain separately proscribed by the statute—the less significant would be the element of duration or persistence over time. On the other hand, depending on the circumstances, a level of physical distress or discomfort that is lacking in extreme intensity may not constitute "severe physical suffering" regardless of its duration—i.e., even if it lasts for a very long period of time. In defining conduct proscribed by sections 2340-2340A, Congress established a high bar. The ultimate question is whether the conduct "is sufficiently extreme and outrageous to warrant the universal condemnation that the term 'torture' both connotes and invokes." *See Price v. Socialist People's Libyan Arab Jamahiriya,* 294 F.3d at 92 (interpreting the TVPA); *cf. Mehinovic v. Vuckovic,* 198 F. Supp. 2d at 1332-40, 1345-46 (standard met under the TVPA by a course of conduct that included severe beatings to the genitals, head, and other parts of the body with metal pipes and various other items; removal of teeth with pliers; kicking in the face and ribs; breaking of bones and ribs and dislocation of fingers; cutting a figure into the victim's forehead; hanging the victim and beating him; extreme limitations of food and water; and subjection to games of "Russian roulette").

This is a verbatim excerpt of a legal memorandum dated May 10, 2005 and submitted to the CIA by the Office of Legal Counsel of the United States Department of Justice. The TVPA is the Torture Victim Protection Act of 1991, a statute that allows for the filing of civil suits, in the U.S., against individuals who, acting in an official capacity for any foreign nation, committed torture.

This memo, signed by then Acting Assistant Attorney General Steven Bradbury, is one of a series of opinions developed by the Office of Legal Counsel to provide legal cover for the Bush Administration's torture program. These memos are available online: *www.aclu.org/accountability.*

PARAGRAPHS

Reza Baraheni

1

A dictator is a beast
Who walks from himself to himself
In between
He shakes hands with beheaded ghosts

2

When the Queen shook hands with me
She looked at my throat
Too thin or too thick, she thought
I assured her that I was regular size
She nodded and we were finished

3

He was told never to look back
Ever since
He has not looked back
But he has never looked ahead either
Our double-headed Orpheus walks around himself

Reza Baraheni was arrested and imprisoned in Tehran in 1973; he spent 102 days in solitary confinement. He later served on the Freedom to Write Committee of PEN American Center and as president of PEN Canada.

4

In the court he sits after the clown
The clown sits after the scribe
The scribe sits after the minister
The minister sits after the king
The king sits after God
God sits after no one
He smiles with one eye to the poet
With the other to the clown
The poet sits after no one
He doesn't even smile to God
The clown smiles to the crown
The minister smiles to the scribe
The scribe smiles to you

5

I've put the ladder against the wall
I've climbed the ladder to the last rung
Take the ladder away
I'll sit on the wall forever
And watch the camels of the young prince go by
Shall I report what I see?
The prince is blind
The camels are lame
The camel men are dumb
And the desert is endless
My wisdom shows me only this
And bells that don't ring
I'll sit on the wall forever

6

Rumi's eyes journey from city to city
His body squats by the gates of the big city
The eyes will go back to the body one day
Be patient

Don't let the young pony catch cold
Cover the doors and windows with rugs and blankets
Sit inside and wait
The eyes will go back to the body one day

7

The gate with the rotten wood is still there
The dog is frozen to stone
The wolf is bleeding wax and steel
Men pass, exchanging slaps
And I'm not ashamed to be here in exile
When women die in hell
And pimps shoot the stars in the name of poets
When houses refuse to stand
And the whole world is covered with sand

8

Poor General Zandipour
He's dead and I live
He presided over the Committee of Rape
He smoked his opium in prison
His wife was fucked by other executioners
—The hand that gives is the hand that takes away—
Birds sing outside prison walls every evening
The torture chambers are full
He would have rejoiced to see his killers tortured
Poor General Zandipour!
He's dead and I live

9

There's nothing softer than the deer's neck to the panther
The reality of the struggle escapes us
We only see a picture and scattered entrails
On the road to the spring

The hunter knows only the road
The shining fur in the sun blinds him
To the identity of the animal
The name escapes him
He sweats and forgets, he sweats
And forgets his mission
While vultures reel around the carcass
And snakes escape from the smell
And the sun sets and the panther
Sleeps
And other panthers sleep

10

Whoever gathers the breeze
From the tops of the trees
Will find the same grace
God is supposed to have
Given to prophets and saints

For:
God is an abstract
Miser who doesn't give
Anything to anyone
A man collects his grace
From the knees of women
And the tops of the trees

FICTION

IMPROVISATION WITH TREES

Alejandro Zambra

Translated by Megan McDowell

1

For now Verónica is someone who does not arrive, who still hasn't returned from her drawing class. Verónica is someone who is lightly absent in the blue room—the blue room is Daniela's bedroom, and the white room is Verónica and Julián's room. There is, in addition, a green room, which they call the guest room as a joke, since it wouldn't be easy to sleep in that mess of books, folders, and paintbrushes. They've set up the big trunk, which several months ago stored their summer clothes, to act as an uncomfortable sofa.

The last hours of a regular day have settled into an established routine: Julián and Verónica leave the blue room when Daniela falls asleep, and later, in the guest room, Verónica draws and Julián reads. Every once in a while she interrupts him or he interrupts her, and these mutual interferences compose dialogues, light conversations, or sometimes important, decisive ones. Later they move to the white room, where they watch television or make love, or start to argue, nothing serious, nothing that can't be fixed immediately, before finishing the movie or when one of them gives up, wanting to sleep or have sex. The usual end to those fights is a fast and silent copulation, or maybe a long one replete with moans and laughter. Then come five or six hours of sleep. And then the next day begins.

But this night is not a regular night, at least not yet. It's still not completely certain that there will be a next day, since Verónica hasn't come back from her drawing class. For now Verónica is absent in the blue room, where Julián distracts the little girl with a story about the private lives of trees.

Right now, sheltered by the solitude of the park, the trees are commenting on the bad luck of an oak, in whose bark two people have carved their names as a symbol of their friendship. No one has the right to give you a tattoo without your consent, says the poplar. The baobab is even more emphatic: The oak has been the victim of a deplorable act of vandalism. Those people deserve punishment. I will not rest until they receive the punishment they deserve. I will traverse earth, sky, and sea in their pursuit.

The little girl laughs hard, without the least sign of sleepiness. And she asks the inevitable questions, never just one, always at least two or three, asked urgently, anxiously: "What's vandalism, Julián? Can you bring me a glass of lemonade, with three sugar cubes? Did you and my mother ever carve your names in a tree, as a symbol of your friendship?"

Julián answers patiently, trying to respect the order of the questions: "Vandalism is what vandals do, vandals are people who do damage just for the joy of doing damage. And yes, I can bring you a glass of lemonade. And no, your mother and I never carved our names in the bark of a tree."

He sees Daniela sleeping and he imagines himself, at eight years old, sleeping. It's automatic; he sees a blind man and imagines himself blind, he reads a good poem and imagines himself writing it, or reading it, aloud, to nobody, impelled by the dark sound of the words. Julián simply accepts these images, receives them and then forgets them. Perhaps he has always limited himself to following images: he hasn't made decisions, hasn't won or lost, but has just let himself be drawn in by certain images, and followed them, without fear or courage, until he got close to them or shut them out.

Stretched out on the bed in the white room, Julián lights a cigarette, the last one, the next to last, or perhaps the first one of a long night, immensely long, consigned by fate to go over the good and bad of a past that is, frankly, blurry. For now, life is a chaos that seems to be resolved: he has been welcomed into a new intimacy, into a world where his role is to be something like a father to Daniela, the sleeping little girl, and a husband to Verónica, the woman who hasn't come back, yet, from her drawing class. From here the story dissipates and there is almost no way to continue it; for now, though, Julián manages a kind of distance from which to watch, attentively, with legitimate interest, the rerun of an old match between Inter and Reggina. It's clear that, any minute now, Inter will score, and Julián doesn't want to miss it, not for anything.

Verónica was in her second year studying for an art degree when Daniela arrived to throw everything off.

Anticipating the pain was her way of experiencing the pain—a young pain, that grew and grew, and sometimes, when the temperature got especially warm, tended to disappear. During the first weeks of her pregnancy she decided to keep the news to herself; she didn't tell Fernando or her best friend, although she didn't have, exactly, a best friend. Verónica and Fernando got married, ready to fulfill the conventions of a happy life. They had decided to put on hold, for a time, their differences, as if they really were a couple and not just a pale idea that took on form despite the bad omens. "I don't want to be a student-pregnant woman. I don't want to be a mother-student," she thought. She definitely didn't want to find herself, in a few months, enfolded in a wide and very flowered dress, explaining to the professor that she hadn't been able to study for the test, or later, two years on, leaving the baby in the librarians' care. She went into a panic imagining the enraptured faces of the librarians, suddenly converted into faithful guardians of the children of others.

During those weeks she went to dozens of art galleries, shamelessly questioned her professors, and lost many hours letting herself be courted by upper-level students, who, as was to be expected, turned out to be insufferable nice guys—nice guys who claimed to be bad and nevertheless prospered faster than their business manager brothers or their educational psychologist sisters.

Sooner rather than later Verónica found the resentment she was looking for. This was not a world of which she wanted to be a part—this wasn't a world, not even close, of which she *could* be a part. From then on, every time a dark thought about her abandoned vocation knocked her down, she returned to those counter-examples she had hoarded away. Instead of thinking about the healthy disdain for artistic fads some of her professors upheld, she remembered the classes she took from two or three charlatans of the type art departments always seem to retain. And instead of thinking about the honest, true works of some of her classmates, she preferred to return to the galleries where the advanced members of the class exhibited their discoveries.

Young artists perfectly imitated the language of the academy and enthusiastically filled out endless forms for government grants. But the money soon ran out, and the young artists had to resign themselves to giving classes for amateurs, like the classes Verónica takes, in the inhospitable event hall of a nearby municipal building. It's been over an hour since she should have been back from her drawing class. "Surely she's on her way," thinks Julián, while he watches TV. Then, in minute 88, against all odds, la Reggina makes the goal, one to nothing. And that's how the game ends: Inter 0, Reggina 1.

Last week Julián turned thirty years old. The party was a bit odd, marred by the gloominess of the guest of honor. In the same way that some women subtract years from their real age, he sometimes has to add a few years on, and pretend to look at the past with a tinge of bitterness. Lately he has started to think he should have been a dentist or geologist or meteorologist. For now, his actual job seems strange: professor. But his true calling, he thinks now, is to have dandruff. He imagines himself answering that way:

"What do you do?"

"I have dandruff."

He's exaggerating, of course. No one can live without exaggerating a little. If there are in fact stages in Julián's life, they would have to be expressed according to an index of exaggeration. Until he was ten years old he exaggerated very little, almost never. From ten to sixteen he steadily increased his pretension. From eighteen onward he became an expert in the most varied forms of exaggeration. Since he's been with Verónica the exaggeration has decreased considerably, in spite of natural relapses that overtake him.

He is professor of literature at four universities in Santiago. He would have liked to stick to one specialty, but the law of supply and demand has forced him to be versatile. He teaches classes in American literature and in Spanish-American literature and even Italian poetry, in spite of the fact that he does not speak Italian. He has read, closely, Ungaretti, Montale, Pavese, Pasolini, and more recent poets, like Patrizia Cavalli and Valerio Magrelli, but in no way is he a specialist in Italian poetry. In any case, in Chile it's not terribly scandalous to teach classes in Italian poetry without knowing Italian, as Santiago is full of English professors who don't know English, and dentists who hardly know how to pull a tooth—and overweight personal trainers, and yoga teachers who could never manage to give classes without a generous dose of antidepressants. Julián tends to clear the bar in his pedagogical adventures. He always salvages a situation by disguising some quotation by Walter Benjamin or Borges or Nicanor Parra.

He is a professor, and a writer on Sundays. There are some weeks when he works as much as possible, obsessively, as if he had a deadline he couldn't miss. This is the time he calls his busy season. Normally, in any case, in the slow season, he puts off his literary ambitions for Sundays, the way other men devote their Sundays to gardening or carpentry or alcoholism.

He has just finished a very short book, which nevertheless took several years to write. At first he gathered materials. He accumulated almost three hundred pages, but gradually discarded more and more, as if instead of adding stories he wanted to subtract them or erase them. The result is paltry: an emaci-ated sheaf of forty-seven pages that he insists on calling a novel. Even though this afternoon he decided to let the book rest for a few weeks, he has turned off the TV and begun, again, to read the manuscript.

Now he reads, he is reading. He tries to pretend he doesn't know the story, and at times he achieves that illusion—he lets himself be carried along innocently, shyly, convincing himself that the text before his eyes was written by someone else. A misplaced comma or a harsh sound, however, and he returns to reality; he is then, again, an author, the author of something, a kind of self-policeman who sanctions his own mistakes, his excesses, his inhibitions. He reads standing up, walking around the room: He should sit or lie down, but he remains stand-ing, his back straight, and he avoids approaching the light, as if afraid to reveal fresh mistakes in the manuscript.

The first image is of a young man conscientiously tending a bonsai. If someone were to ask him for a summary of his book, he would probably respond that it was about a young man conscientiously tending a bonsai. Maybe he wouldn't say a young man, maybe he would limit himself to the statement that the protagonist is not exactly a boy or a mature adult or an old man. One night, many years ago now, he mentioned the image to his friends Sergio and Bernardita: a man locked in with his bonsai, tending it, moved by the possibil-ity of a real work of art. A few days later they gave him, as an in-joke, a tiny elm. "So you can write your book," they told him.

2

Daniela wakes up. She always wakes up at midnight and it has just struck twelve. With a muted and tearful voice she asks Julián to tuck her in again. "Your mom will be home soon," says Julián. "She just called, she's fine, she had to go to the hospital with a friend. A pregnant friend who was having contrac-tions," he clarifies. And he adds, "They had two flat tires on the way there."

The little girl doesn't know the word contractions, and she also doesn't know that having two flat tires is very unusual, but Daniela isn't worried about her mother's lateness, or not exactly. She just wants Julián to stay with her, wants him to tuck her in again, wants him to defend her from the dark.

"I don't know why all children are afraid of the dark. At your age I wasn't afraid of the dark," he says, and it's a lie, or maybe it's the truth: when Julián was a child he wasn't afraid of the darkness itself, but rather the possibility of going blind. One night he woke up and saw not a glimmer of light anywhere: first he had the impression that someone had *locked* him in the room, then the dreadful conviction that he had gone blind. Since then he cannot bear absolute darkness, locked rooms.

"Do you want another story of 'The Private Lives of Trees?'"

"Yes," answers Daniela. And Julián assents, reluctantly, since his eyes are hurting, or his ears, he isn't sure. He would like to fall asleep, suddenly and irresponsibly, and wake up tomorrow, or yesterday, like new. It has to be a short story, only the beginning, until the girl falls asleep again—maybe the story of a giant who takes care of the trees as if they were plants in a little garden, or the adventure of a little boy who climbed up an oak and didn't want to come down ever again. Julián foresees that the narration is going to get tangled up. Maybe it's better to improvise, he thinks, maybe the only thing that makes sense is to improvise:

The poplar and the baobab are talking about the crazy people who visit the park. They agree, beforehand, that there are a lot of crazy people who go to the park. The park is full of crazies, but my personal favorite crazy person, says the baobab, is a woman with very long arms who came to talk to me one time. I remember it like it was yesterday, although it was long ago, I must have been barely two hundred fifteen or two hundred twenty when she came, you hadn't even been born yet.

Immediately Julián realizes he has made a mistake: Daniela awakes from her doze, surprised by the poplar's age, and especially because she thought that the poplar and the baobab had always lived together, that's why they were such good friends, because they had spent their lives planted in the park together. To get out of it, he makes up a nervous string of dates, from which is gathered that the baobab is one thousand five hundred years old and the poplar barely forty. Daniela is still confused and Julián continues, conscious that he will have to work hard to recuperate the tale.

It was, says the baobab, a woman with very long arms. At first I thought she was a little girl, because she had braces, but it wasn't a little girl, it was a woman with very long arms that reached the ground. A woman who was not exactly beautiful, but very unusual: green eyes, short white hair, dark skin, and thick braces between her teeth, and those long arms that touched the ground. She was or she had been a painter, and her name was Otoko.

Julián has decided to concentrate on the crazy woman, although now he isn't thinking of her as a crazy woman, but rather as a lonely woman or a woman who talks to herself, talks to trees. He tries out, then, Otoko's monologue before the old baobab:

I'm a painter, says Otoko, but now I have a problem and I have to stop being a painter. The problem is my arms, which have grown so much. It's very difficult to paint with such long arms, my eyes get tired, the canvas is far away, I can barely focus on it.

I got a prescription for glasses, but I don't plan on using them, at least not until they take my braces off. Since I was a little girl my motto was: glasses or braces. I chose braces, how was I to know that my arms would get so long and I wouldn't be able to paint and all that.

It's not very common for a person's arms to grow so much. Branches yes, branches grow, you know that better than I, baobab. Branches grow until they die all of a sudden, but it's not very common for a person's arms to grow so much.

It's not common but maybe it's not so strange, either. Maybe I'm one in a thousand or one in a million, and I like that, it's a privilege. It's a problem and a privilege.

So I'm going to look for another job. I plan on collecting leaves from the ground, since it's easy for me, I don't even have to bend over. I will wander through the parks all day collecting leaves from the ground.

Although it's not necessary, since Daniela has gone back to sleep, Julián continues the story, but now the one speaking is not the painter or leaf collector, but another woman, more beautiful than Otoko or at least with not such long arms, with normal ones. It's not Verónica, not by any means is it Verónica, who is still rambling along some faraway avenue. Somehow, Verónica is the only woman who could not figure into the story that Julián is improvising aloud, for nobody, for the little girl asleep.

3

It's four in the morning and Julián reconsiders a possibility that earlier he had denied entirely: Verónica is not detained in a distant avenue, but rather in the house of a man who this time has convinced her to not go home. He composes the picture, doesn't avoid the details. He imagines the damp walls and the light of a paraffin stove illuminating the lovers, who are not posing, they don't have time to stop and wave to the camera. There is a smell of orange peel or incense, of perfume worn out by the friction of bodies—Verónica's shining thighs and her firm, hot skin.

"It's not a house," thinks Julián. He takes a long second to create, instead, an eye-catching room, replete with mirrors, a fountain emitting a subtle artificial noise. He imagines Verónica dulled by a rough whiskey, topped off with a few lines of coke, moving, with no hurry, on top of someone. It's a round explanation, unquestionable: Verónica hasn't come home yet because she is in bed with her drawing teacher, it was a quick screw that became a long one. It happens. Right now the drawing teacher or grammar or quantum physics teacher is penetrating her for the sixth or seventh time. "Don't worry," says Julián out loud. "Don't worry, I already put the little girl to sleep, I already told her a story, don't rush, just keep on fucking, go right ahead, fucking bitch, you can still suck him off one last time."

But this is not one of those game shows where you have to dress up as a beggar and survive the ridicule of others. Not even by fanning the flames of a horrible conjecture can Julián change the plot; he is sure this is not the reason for his wife's lateness. The image of Verónica lost in a distant avenue becomes huge, turns into a kind of truth.

He is stretched out on the floor, like a lion in its cage—more like a cat, or like those weird and horrible fish that the little girl chose out of pity a few months ago. "If we get out of this," thinks Julián, "we'll save some money and go on vacation to Valdivia or Puerto Montt, or maybe it's better not to hope for too much: If we get out of this we will go, on Saturday, finally, to see the snow." He had discarded the idea, motivated by an old class resentment, but now he thinks about it again. The Chilean snows are for the rich, he knows that very well, but he has already gotten used to coexisting with people far removed from him, who after a while become friendly. Right away the plan breaks down, it could not last. He has discovered, in his own wording, a deep fissure: We will not get out of this. To get out of this would mean Verónica crossing, as though nothing had happened, a threshold that has been closed for hours. To get out of this would mean, perhaps, waking up. But he can't wake up: He is awake.

Even so, he keeps thinking about the snow, a spectral space, relegated to novels: a world where young people fall gravely ill and old people remember their past loves. The snow is a crude and beautiful fraud. He would like to see—to have seen, throughout his life—the snow. At eighteen years old, for example, to have gotten on a bus, to have taken a job in the kitchen of a five-star hotel, taking orders from a black chef, a recently retired soldier, surely. He imagines himself looking up from below, from the snow, at a ski lift full of tiny tourists.

He approaches the wall of the white room. He tries to decide, with an absurd seriousness, whether the wall is white like winter or white like snow. He doesn't know if it's possible to paint a wall the color of snow. He has never seen snow. He closes his eyes and puts pressure on his eyelids for twenty, thirty seconds. And he returns, cautious, fearful, to this story of hard facts, which at times resembles a book on how to paint. There are three rooms, and three small popular libraries: blue, white, green, beige, red, and brown. Arturo Prat Street is brown. Chilean literature is brown. The room is white and maybe the snow, too, is white. The streets are not white: the streets are light blue or dark blue, sea green, emerald green, red, pink, yellow: Ahumada is red, Recoleta is pink, and Tobalaba, the street parallel to the passage where he lives now, is sky blue, the same as Bilbao. Diez de Julio and Vicuña Mackenna are orange-colored streets.

4

Daniela thinks about her mother, who is alive, or is dead. It's still not clear.

Maybe one night she just didn't come back. It was Julián who told her "she won't be coming back," or "she died," or "something very bad happened, something very sad." Now Daniela thinks about her mother, and then about her father. She wants to see them. And she chooses well; she chooses to visit her father.

After lunch with her father, however, Daniela decides to read her stepfather's novel. It's easy to find the book: on the same shelf as always, where it's always been, sheltered by an impassive alphabetical order. For many years she lacked the curiosity and maybe the bravery to read it. Now, when she opens it, she finds this message on the inside cover: "To Daniela, with love, hoping it doesn't bore you."

She recognizes her stepfather's handwriting—the letters gone over with care, as if fighting the slight shake that all the same has been impressed onto the paper. "A smoker's writing," she thinks, although there's no such thing as a smoker's writing. Ready to be swept up by solitude, Daniela is astonished to recognize, with such precision, Julián's writing. She never saw him write by hand, she just remembers him smoking, in front of the computer, typing at a speed that at the time seemed enviable; then, five seconds later, he would erase just as fast the words he had written.

She should go to the park or to the airport, to look for something, to wait for someone. But she chose to stay home, instigating a trickle of memories. She acts as if she had been requested to stay home. She reads as if reading were an act of obedience, as if she had to write a summary, a school composition: forty-five minutes, timed, to respond to a single, unfair question. How does one read a stepfather's book?

Julián's novel is so short that a half hour would suffice to read it. But Daniela stops every page and a half to make coffee, to see if the coffee is ready, to pour a cup of coffee, and then she pauses every time she takes a sip, and after every sip she looks at the ceiling, or lights a cigarette, and begins to stop after every drag, too. She needs silence so she can hear her sips of coffee and drags on the cigarette. She needs silence to watch the smoke disperse in the stream of light from the window.

She doesn't get bored, or not too bored. She hopes to find, in the book, features of herself, flashes of a remote past, of a time she surely lived through but remembers with difficulty. She doesn't have childhood memories. She wouldn't be able to relate her life story: there are scarcely a few bare scenes which cross and recross her memory. They are pieces which only after enormous effort could constitute a history, a life.

But she searches, she searches: maybe from one paragraph to another there were days, weeks, or months. Maybe she came in, unexpected, while Julián was writing, and from that interruption was left, in the book, a phrase or at least a word. So she marks some fragments, which are not the ones that she likes best, but the phrases that maybe she said and Julián stole, copied from her. She is happy, she lets herself be swept along by the mirage that in this book beats her own language, Daniela's own.

It's a love story, nothing all that unusual. Two people construct, freely and deliberately and guilelessly, a parallel world that, naturally, very soon goes under. It's the story of a mediocre, juvenile love, in which she recognizes her own class: narrow apartments, half-truths, automatic words of love, cowardice and fanaticism, illusions lost and later found again—the abrupt changes of fate of those who go up and down but don't go or stay. Fleeting words, words that anticipate a revelation that never arrives.

There are no parallel worlds, Daniela knows that very well. She has survived mediocrity; "I'm ready for anything," she liked to say a few years ago. And it was true. She was ready for anything, whatever, to accept whatever she was given, to say whatever it was necessary to say. But not anymore. Now she is not ready for anything. Now she is free.

Daniela finishes reading and immediately returns to the passages she has marked. She searches for her language, searches for herself, but doesn't find anything. She isn't in the book. She got lost. And it doesn't displease her, this absence. Invaded by a mixture of relief and disappointment, she closes the book. Her life has not changed. Probably tomorrow she will reread it to confirm her impressions. But she isn't going to remember any story that gives some sense to the present, to the past, to the future. She doesn't want to cheat. Her life has not changed: she doesn't know any more or any less. She doesn't feel any more or any less.

Is it easier to read a stepfather's book than a father's book? She must think about gardens, women who talk to nobody, changing a tire in a faraway avenue. She must think about the fragile beauty of sick trees. She must imagine a park covered in fallen awnings. She must conjecture about the solitude of a man confined to the four walls of a damp apartment, a man who has refused to say the lines he is given.

Julián would have liked her to remember the stories about trees, or the torturous hours that they spent memorizing multiplication tables, that sententious, pedagogical tone he sometimes used. Julián would have liked for Daniela to remember him after reading his book. But no. Memory is no refuge. There remains only an inconsistent babble of street names that no longer exist.

It is nighttime.

Daniela opens the windows, since she wants to sleep hearing the footsteps, barks, horns, security alarms, the neighbors' conversations. She thinks about herself, when she was a little girl who pretended to sleep while Julián read and her mother painted. Little by little, sleep overtakes her.

Now she is sleeping. She is asleep.

DANCING DAY I

Marie Ponsot

At the horizon's lit fog rim
earth keeps in touch with sky.
I call this the end of the beginning.

In its mist, frayed ghosts of selves drowse;
I call them my lost selves.
Lately they drift close, unaging,
watching me age. Now & then, one or some

flare up, known shapes in known clothes.
Each of them is not not me, and wears
the clothes I walked in, joked, worked hurt in,

as I played my sweet pipsqueak part
paradiddle on the high hat.
I still know all those moves.

I begin to remember; I remember them,
some from when my father was alive.
A deep breath taken. Restorative.
They hum soft part-songs, hard to hear.
And now they're singing. They've come to stay!
It's turning into a party.

I put out bread, plates, glasses, grapes,
apples, napkins, pretzels, Bleu des Causses.

MARIE PONSOT | 197

They whistle old signals. In our one name
we agree to our selving. I do agree.
                              I'll propose a toast,
why not. Time to let go. Get going.
Out of the cellar I take, ripe,
the rest of the case of Clos de Vougeot.

DANCING DAY II

Marie Ponsot

Once, one made many.
Now, many make one.
The rest is requiem.

We're running out of time, so
we're hurrying home to
practice to
gether for the general dance.
We're past get-ready, almost at get-set.
Here we come many to
dance as one.

Plenty more lost selves keep arriving, some
we weren't waiting for. We stretch and
lace up practice shoes. We mind our manners—
no staring, just snatching a look
      —strict and summative—
at each other's feet & gait & port.

Every one we ever were shows up
with world-flung poor triumphs
flat in the back-packs we set down to greet
each other. Glad tired gaudy
we are more than we thought
& as ready as we'll ever be.

We've all learned the moves, separately,

from the absolute dancer
    the foregone deep breather
the original choreographer.

Imitation's limitation—but who cares.
We'll be at our best on dancing day.
    On dancing day
we'll belt out tunes we'll step to
together
till it's time for us to say
there's nothing more to say
nothing to pay   no way
pay no mind   pay no heed
pay as we go.
Many is one; we're out of here,
exeunt omnes

      exit   oh and save
      this last dance for me

on the darkening ground
looking up into
the last hour of left light
in the star-stuck east,
its vanishing flective, bent
breathlessly.

CONTRIBUTORS

Chimamanda Ngozi Adichie grew up in Nigeria and moved to the United States at the age of nineteen. Her novel *Purple Hibiscus* was awarded the Commonwealth Writers' Prize for Best First Book. *Half of a Yellow Sun* won the Orange Prize for Fiction and a PEN Beyond Margins Award. Her latest book, *The Thing Around Your Neck*, is a collection of stories.

Rabih Alameddine is the author of a story collection, *The Perv*, and three novels: *The Hakawati, Koolaids: The Art of War*, and *I, the Divine*. He has published fiction and nonfiction in numerous publications and is the recipient of a Guggenheim fellowship. He is also a painter. He was born in Jordan and lives in San Francisco and Beirut.

Khaled al-Berry was born in Sohag, Egypt. As a teenager, he joined a radical Islamist group. He began to question his beliefs after discovering literature at Cairo University. "The Call" is an excerpt from his memoir, *Life Is More Beautiful Than Paradise*, which will be published in December. He now lives in London.

Meena Alexander is the author of several works of literary criticism, fiction, and poetry, including *Illiterate Heart*, winner of a PEN Beyond Margins Award, and *Raw Silk*. Her first poems were published when she was a teenager in Sudan. She teaches at Hunter College and the CUNY Graduate Center. *Poets of Dislocation* will be published in November.

Kazim Ali is the author of three novels and two books of poetry. *The Far Mosque*, a collection of poems, received the Alice James Books' New England/New York Award. He is the founding editor of Nightboat Books and teaches at Oberlin College and the Stonecoast MFA Program.

Benjamin Anastas is the author of two novels, *An Underachiever's Diary* and *The Faithful Narrative of a Pastor's Disappearance*. His work has been published in *The Paris Review, GQ, Bookforum*, and *The New York Times Magazine*, among other publications. He lives in Brooklyn and Tuscany.

Kwame Anthony Appiah is the President of PEN American Center. He is the author of three novels and many scholarly titles, and his essays and reviews appear regularly in the *New York Review of Books*. He won the 2007 Arthur Ross Book Award from the Council on Foreign Relations for *Cosmopolitanism: Ethics in a World of Strangers*. He teaches at Princeton and is working on *The Life of Honor: An Essay in the Genealogy of Morals*.

Nadeem Aslam was born in Pakistan and immigrated to the United Kingdom at fourteen. His novels include *Maps for Lost Lovers*, which received the 2005 Kiriyama Prize, and *Season of the Rainbirds*, which received a Betty Trask Award and the Authors' Club First Novel Award. His latest novel is *The Wasted Vigil*. He lives in London.

Reza Baraheni is the author of more than sixty books of poetry, fiction, literary theory, and criticism, and co-founder of the Writers Association of Iran. He was targeted and imprisoned by the Shah's regime in Iran, and moved to the United States, where he worked on PEN's Freedom to Write Committee. He was granted asylum by Canada and served as president of PEN Canada. He lives and teaches in Toronto.

Nathaniel Bellows is a novelist, poet, and essayist. His books include *On This Day* and *Why Speak?* His work has appeared in numerous publications, including *The New York Times Book Review*, *The Paris Review*, and *The New Republic*. He lives in New York.

J.M.G. Le Clézio was born in Nice in 1940. His first novel, *The Interrogation*, won the Renaudot Prize. He has written more than forty works of fiction and nonfiction and lives in Mauritius, Nice, and Albuquerque, where he teaches literature at the University of New Mexico. He received the Nobel Prize for literature in 2008.

Cynthia Cruz is a poet whose work has appeared in *The Paris Review*, *The American Poetry Review*, and other publications. Her first book, *Ruin*, was published by Alice James Books in 2006. She lives in Brooklyn and teaches at Sarah Lawrence College.

Nilo Cruz, a Cuban-American playwright, was awarded the 2009 PEN/Laura Pels Foundation Award for Drama. In 2003, his play *Anna in the Tropics* received the Pulitzer Prize for Drama. He currently lives in New York City, where he is writing the book of the upcoming musical *Havana*.

Ariel Dorfman grew up in Chile and was forced into exile in 1973. His play *Death and the Maiden* won the Laurence Olivier Award; his most recent books are *Other Septembers, Many Americas*, and *Burning City*. He teaches at Duke University and has divided his time between Santiago and the United States since the restoration of democracy to Chile in 1990.

Brian Evenson is the author of nine works of fiction, including *Father of Lies* and *The Open Curtain*, and the recipient of an O. Henry Prize and a fellowship from the NEA, among other honors. His most recent collection of stories, *Fugue State*, was published in July. He is the director of Brown University's Literary Arts Program.

Richard Ford is the author of six novels and three collections of stories. In 1996, he was awarded the Pulitzer Prize and the PEN/Faulkner Award for his novel *Independence Day*. In 2001, he received the PEN/Malamud Award for excellence in short fiction. His most recent book is *The Lay of the Land*.

Rivka Galchen's debut novel, *Atmospheric Disturbances*, was published in 2008. It was named as a finalist for several awards, including the Canadian Writers' Trust's Fiction Prize and the Governor General's Award. She teaches at Columbia University.

Forrest Gander is a translator, novelist, and poet. His translations include *Firefly Under the Tongue: Selected Poems of Coral Bracho*, which was a finalist for the 2009 PEN Translation Prize. He has received fellowships from the NEA and from the Guggenheim, Whiting, and Howard foundations.

Adam Gopnik has been writing for *The New Yorker* since 1986. His most recent book, *Angels and Ages*, was published in January of this year. He has received the George Polk Award for Magazine Reporting and has won three National Magazine Awards. He is also author of the book *Paris to the Moon*.

Déwé Gorodé was active in the independence movement of New Caledonia and was jailed by French authorities in the 1970s. She became Vice President of the New Caledonian government in 2001. She has published collections of poetry as well as several volumes of short stories, and she continues to write in English, French, and the Kanak language of Paicî.

Philip Gourevitch is the editor of *The Paris Review* and a long-time staff writer for *The New Yorker*. He is the author of *We Wish to Inform You that Tomorrow We Will Be Killed with Our Families: Stories from Rwanda*, winner of the National Book Critics Circle Award and the *Los Angeles Times* Book Prize. *The Ballad of Abu Ghraib*, written with filmmaker Errol Morris, was published earlier this year.

Norbert Gstrein was born in Austria in 1961. His novel *Die englischen Jahre (The English Years)* received the Alfred Döblin Prize, and *Das Handwerk des Tötens (The Craft of Killing)* received the Uwe Johnson Prize. He lives in Hamburg, Germany.

Emmanuel Guibert has written graphic novels for readers of all ages, including the *Sardine in Outer Space* series and *The Professor's Daughter*. His most recent book is *The Photographer*, which has won numerous awards and been translated into languages all over the world. *Alan's War: The Memories of G.I. Alan Cope* was first published in English in 2008.

Christian Hawkey is the author of *The Book of Funnels*, which won the Kate Tufts Discovery Award, a chapbook called *HourHour*, and *Citizen Of*. Among his many honors is a Creative Capital Innovative Literature Award. His next book, *Ventrakl*, will be published in 2010.

Will Heinrich won the PEN/Robert Bingham Fellowship for Writers for his novel *The King's Evil*, which was published in 2003. He has written for *The New York Observer* and other publications. He lives in New York City, where he was born and raised.

Aleksandar Hemon is the author of four books of fiction. *Nowhere Man* was a finalist for the National Books Critics Circle Award, as was *The Lazarus Project*, which was also a finalist for the National Book Award. He has received a Guggenheim Fellowship and a "genius grant" from the MacArthur Foundation. His most recent book, *Love and Obstacles*, is a collection of stories.

Juan Felipe Herrera has published over twenty volumes of poetry, prose, drama, children's books, and young adult novels. The winner of numerous awards and fellowships, he received the 2008 National Book Critics Circle Award in Poetry for *Half the World in Light*. He teaches at University of California, Riverside.

Kabir, c. 1440-1518, was a poet whose work strongly influenced the Bhakti religious movement in India. His writing was rooted in mysticism and religious symbolism, though he apparently refused to identify with any established religion and has been revered by Muslims, Hindus, and Sikhs.

Bożena Keff is a poet, essayist, and cultural critic. She has published three books of poems, two essay collections, and *Postać z cieniem (Figure with a Shadow)*, about Jewish women in Polish literature. She teaches at the University of Warsaw and elsewhere. "Lara Croft" is excerpted from a book-length poem, *On Mother and the Fatherland*.

Jan Kjærstad has received many awards for his work, including the Henrik Steffen Prize, awarded to Scandinavians who have enriched the intellectual and artistic life of Europe. *The Discoverer*, the third book in his Wergeland trilogy—which also includes *The Seducer* and *The Conqueror*—was recently published in English.

Amitava Kumar has written numerous works of nonfiction, fiction, and poetry, including *Bombay–London–New York*. His novel *Home Products* was short-listed for the Crossword Book Award. His forthcoming book *A Foreigner Carrying in the Crook of His Arm a Tiny Bomb* is a writer's report on the global war on terror. He teaches at Vassar College.

Peter Kuper is the co-founder of the political zine *World War 3 Illustrated* and has been drawing "Spy vs. Spy" for *Mad* magazine since 1997. His latest book, *Diario de Oaxaca*, is a sketchbook journal of two years he spent in Mexico.

Nam Le was born in Vietnam and raised in Australia. *The Boat*, a collection of stories, won the Dylan Thomas Prize and was named the best debut of 2008 by *New York Magazine*. It was also selected as a *New York Times* Notable Book. Le is the fiction editor of the *Harvard Review*.

Sara Majka received an MFA from Bennington. She has published stories in *Zone 3*, *A Public Space*, and *H.O.W.*, and has a story forthcoming in *The Massachusetts Review*.

She is currently a fellow at the Provincetown Fine Arts Work Center.

Pasha Malla is a poet and fiction writer. His story collection *The Withdrawal Method* won the Trillium Book Award, the Danuta Gleed Literary Prize, and was chosen as a *Globe and Mail* and *National Post* book of the year. His fiction has won the Arthur Ellis Award for crime writing and he has been published in two *Journey Prize* anthologies. His first novel, *People Park*, will be published in 2010.

Jaime Manrique is a novelist, poet, journalist, and teacher born in Barranquilla, Colombia. His first poetry collection, *Latin Moon in Manhattan*, won Colombia's National Poetry Award. Other works include *Eminent Maricones* and *Our Lives Are the Rivers*. He has received a Guggenheim Foundation Fellowship, among other awards. He teaches at Columbia University.

Colum McCann was born in Dublin and teaches at Hunter College in New York. His fiction has been published in thirty languages and has appeared in *The New Yorker*, *The Atlantic Monthly*, and *GQ*. His most recent novel, *Let the Great World Spin*, was published in June; an excerpt appeared in *PEN America 10: Fear Itself*.

Albert Mobilio is a critic and poet. He has won the National Book Critics Circle Award for Excellence in Reviewing, a Gertrude Stein Award for Innovative Writing, and a Whiting Writer's Award. His books include *The Geographics* and *Letters from Mayhem*. A co-editor of *Bookforum*, he is currently a writer-in-residence at the New School.

Sigrid Nunez is the author of five novels, most recently *The Last of Her Kind*. *A Feather on the Breath of God* was a finalist for the PEN/Hemingway Award. "Rapture Children" is excerpted from her sixth novel, *Salvation City*, which will be published in the fall of 2010. She lives in New York City.

The Office of Legal Counsel of the United States Department of Justice was created in 1934 by an act of the United States Congress. It assists the Attorney General of the United States in his or her function as legal adviser to the President and to all the executive branch agencies.

Cynthia Ozick is a short story writer, novelist, playwright, and essayist. In 2008, she was awarded the PEN/Malamud Award for her short stories and the PEN/Nabokov Award for a body of work of "enduring originality and consummate craftsmanship." Her many books include *The Shawl* and *The Puttermesser Papers*. Her most recent book, a work of fiction, is *Dictation: A Quartet*.

Ed Park is a founding editor of *The Believer*. His fiction and nonfiction have appeared in numerous publications and his novel *Personal Days* was a finalist for the PEN/ Hemingway Award and the John Sargent Sr. First Novel Prize. It was also named one of *Time*'s Top Ten Fiction Books of the year. He lives in New York.

Marie Ponsot is a poet, literary critic, essayist, teacher, and translator. Her poetry collection *The Bird Catcher* won a National Book Critics Circle Award, and *Springing: New and Selected Poems* was named a *New York Times* Notable Book. She teaches at the Poetry Center of the 92nd Street Y in New York City. Her latest poetry collection is *Easy.*

Roxana Robinson has written four novels, three story collections, and a biography of Georgia O'Keeffe. Four of her books have been named *New York Times* Notable Books, and she has received fellowships from the NEA and the Guggenheim Foundation. She lives in New York and Maine.

Damion Searls is a writer and a translator. His book of stories *What We Were Doing and Where We Were Going* was published this year, as were his selections and translations of Rilke and Proust and two books that he edited: an abridgment of Thoreau's *Journal* and an experimental version of Melville's *Moby-Dick* entitled *; or the Whale.*

Roger Sedarat is a poet. His collection *Dear Regime: Letters to the Islamic Republic* won the 2007 Hollis Summer Poetry Prize. He has also published a chapbook, *From Tehran to Texas.* He has a book forthcoming on landscape in recent New England poetry. He teaches at Queens College.

David Shields is the author of nine books, including *The Thing About Life Is That One Day You'll Be Dead,* a *New York Times* bestseller. He has won numerous awards, including the PEN Syndicated Fiction Award for his novel *Dead Languages.* "Mimesis" is excerpted from his upcoming book, *Reality Hunger: A Manifesto,* which will be published in February 2010. He lives in Seattle.

Scott Spencer has written eight novels, including *Endless Love* and *A Ship Made of Paper.* Both were National Book Award Finalists. His nonfiction has appeared in *Rolling Stone, The New York Times,* and *The New Yorker,* among other publications. He lives in upstate New York.

Jayne Lyn Stahl is a poet, essayist, playwright, and screenwriter. Her poetry has appeared in *The New York Quarterly* and *City Lights Review,* and she was a finalist for the PEN/Joyce Osterweil Award for Poetry in 2006. She is the founder of Writers-at-Large, a free-expression advocacy group.

Mathias Svalina lives in Lincoln, Nebraska, where he is pursuing a PhD in creative writing at the University of Nebraska. His poems have been published in *Willow Springs, River City, Perihelion, La Petite Zine,* and other journals. He is a co-editor of *Octopus Magazine,* and his first book, *Destruction Myth,* has just been published.

Terese Svoboda has published ten books of prose and poetry. Her many honors include a PEN/Columbia Fellowship, an O. Henry Prize, the Bobst Prize in Fiction, the John Golden Award in Playwriting, the Graywolf Nonfiction Prize for *Black Glasses Like Clark Kent*, and the Iowa Poetry Prize for *Laughing Africa*. Her most recent book is *Weapons Grade: Poems*.

Lynne Tillman has published novels, story collections, and works of nonfiction. Her novel *No Lease on Life* was a *New York Times* Notable Book and a finalist for the National Book Critics Circle Award, and she received a Guggenheim Fellowship in 2006. Her most recent novel is *American Genius: A Comedy*.

Nancy Willard is a poet, novelist, essayist, and children's book author. She has published twelve books of poetry, including *Water Walker*, which was nominated for the National Book Critics Circle Award. Her children's book of poems, *A Visit to William Blake's Inn*, was awarded the Newbery Medal. She lives in New York and teaches at Vassar College.

Liu Xiaobo is a poet, essayist, and political activist based in Beijing. He is a former president of the Independent Chinese PEN Center and received the Fondation de France Prize from Reporters Without Borders for the defense of press freedom. He was recently charged with "inciting subversion of state power" and is being held at an undisclosed location in Beijing. If convicted, he faces up to fifteen years in prison.

Alejandro Zambra was born in Santiago, Chile, in 1975. He has published two books of poetry and *Bonsai*, a novella. "Improvisation with Trees" was adapted from his novella *The Private Lives of Trees*. In 2007 he was selected for the "Bogota 39," a selection of the top Latin American writers under the age of 39.

ACKNOWLEDGMENTS

"The Call" is excerpted from *Life Is More Beautiful than Paradise* by Khaled al-Berry, first published in Arabic by Dar al-Nahar as *al-Dunya ajmal min al-janna* in 2001; a revised edition was published by Dar Merit in 2009. Copyright © 2001, 2009 by Khaled al-Berry. English translation copyright © 2009 by Humphrey Davies. *Life Is More Beautiful then Paradise* will be published in November 2009 by the American University in Cairo Press and Arabia Books.

"The Museum of Dreams" is adapted from *Hortensia and the Museum of Dreams*, published in *Two Sisters and a Piano and Other Plays* by Nilo Cruz. Copyright © 2007 by Nilo Cruz. Theatre Communications Group. Reprinted by permission of the author.

"Rebel Sun" was first published in *Sharing as Custom Provides* by Déwé Gorodé, translated and edited by Raylene Ramsay and Deborah Walker. Copyright © 2004 by Déwé Gorodé. Pandanus Books. Reprinted by permission of the author.

Excerpt from *Alan's War: The Memories of G.I. Alan Cope*, by Emmanuel Guibert, published by arrangement with First Second, an imprint of Roaring Brook Press, a division of Holtzbrinck Publishing Holdings Limited Partnership. Copyright © 2000, 2002, 2008 by Emmanuel Guibert & L'Association. English translation copyright © 2008 by First Second. All rights reserved.

"Óyeme, Mamita" from *Half the World in Light* by Juan Felipe Herrera. Copyright © 2008 by Juan Felipe Herrera. The University of Arizona Press. Reprinted by permission of the author.

"The Top" excerpted from *Give It Up! and other short stories* by Peter Kuper. Copyright © 1995 by Peter Kuper. NBM Publishing. Reprinted by permission of the artist.

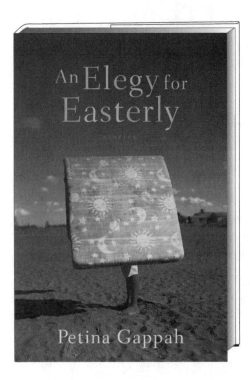

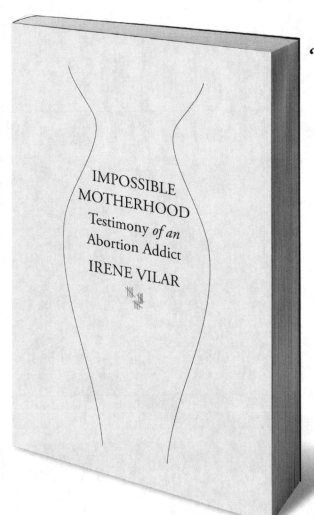

M A N D O R L A

NUEVA ESCRITURA DE LAS AMÉRICAS • NEW WRITING FROM THE AMERICAS

COVER IMAGE FROM ISSUE 12 BY ARTURO ERNESTO ROMO-SANTILLANO

ISSUE 12 –

New writing, translations, visual art, and critical commentaries.

Featuring contributions from:

Sesshu Foster, Arturo Ernesto Romo-Santillano, Rodrigo Toscano, Mario Arteca, Anne Waldman, Raúl Zurita, Daniel Borzutzky, Reynaldo Jiménez, Felipe Cussen, Javier Norambuena, Rodrigo Gómez, Héctor Hernández Montesinos, Achy Obejas, Marcos Canteli, Sérgio Medeiros, Raymond L. Bianchi, Lilliana Ramos Collado, Laird Hunt, Antonio Ochoa, Domingo De Ramos, Urayoán Noel, William Carlos Williams, Hugo García Manríquez, Regina Vater, Paulo Leminski, Iván García, Kath Anderson, Marina Porcelli, James J. Pancrazio, Antonio Benítez Rojo, James E. Maraniss, Óscar David López, Bhanu Kapil, Jessica Díaz, Chris Pusateri, Eliot Weinberger, Román Antopolsky, Kent Johnson, Gabriel Bernal Granados, Sawako Nakayasu, Reynaldo Jiménez, Michelle Naka Pierce, Sue Hammond West, Rito Ramón Aroche, María DeGuzmán, José Kozer, Melisa Machado, S.M. Stone, O.M. Ulloa, Omar Pérez, Graham Foust, Claire Becker, Gabriel Andrés Eljaiek Rodríguez, Jorge Camacho

Mandorla *is available to libraries through Ebsco and to bookstores through Ubiquity Distributors or Ingram* *Distribution. For individual subscriptions, contact Sarah Haberstich at skhaber@ilstu.edu.*

THE LITERARY REVIEW

WWW.THELITERARYREVIEW.ORG

AN INTERNATIONAL
JOURNAL OF
CONTEMPORARY
WRITING

MANIFEST DESTINY

Featuring: Politics, culture, self-invention, the determined combination of will and imaginations, brute force, gale force, war, the inevitable, hybridity, plowing forward, skipping past, ideology, territory, visionary, guns, saints, a twitching heart.

Featuring: Ilan Stavans, Kelly Cherry, Michiah Bay Gualt, Huan Hsu, Eric-Emmanuel Schmitt, Matt Mendez, Thomas Reither, Martin Jude Farawell, Nina Berberova, Jerald Walker, Paul Ruffin, Renee Ashley, Robert Polito

SUMMER 2009

PEN is the first organization of any kind I have ever joined.
Let's hope I don't regret it!

— Henry Miller, 1957

JOIN PEN!

Associate Membership in PEN American Center is open to everyone who supports PEN's mission and wants to play a vital role in supporting and furthering PEN's efforts on behalf of writers and readers both at home and abroad. The benefits of Associate Membership include:

* a subscription to *PEN America*, our award-winning semiannual journal

* discounted access to the online database Grants and Awards Available to American Writers, the most comprehensive directory of its kind

* select invitations to Member-only receptions

* discounts to public programs, including PEN World Voices: The New York Festival of International Literature

* access to the Associate Member Exchange, an e-bulletin board on the PEN web site where Members can share links, blogs, and homepages

Annual dues are $40 ($20 for students).

Join online at **www.pen.org/join** or write to us at:

PEN American Center
Membership Dept.
588 Broadway, 303
New York, NY 10012